SHOPPING *for* **Vintage**

the definitive guide to vintage fashion

FUNMI ODULATE

illustrations by Richard Merritt

'*This is the most* **comprehensive and inspiring guide** *for those of us who are* **passionate about vintage fashion**. *I can't wait to go on my travels armed with all this insiders' information.*'

LULU GUINNESS

QUADRILLE

Strictly speaking, vintage fashion is clothing that is at least 25 years old. Just a few years ago, this wasn't a fashion slant you leant towards unless preparing for a fancy-dress party. 'Vintage' was simply another word for 'second hand'. Today, the sartorial ethos couldn't be more different as vintage fashion is coveted the world over. Wearing vintage provides an opportunity to sport beautifully made clothes that are individual, a unique piece of history and, many a time, less expensive than their latter-day designer counterparts. As it is less about trends, vintage has a long-lasting appeal that, bolstered by the celebrity patronage of high-profile purveyors such as Kate Moss and Sienna Miller, has exerted a huge influence on the fashion philosophies of the world's style-conscious women.

As pioneers of their time, old-school couturiers commanded a reverence seldom found today. During those eras of elegance, the craftsmanship employed in the clothes reflected the regard in which glamour and finesse were held. The current interest in past fashion houses arguably signifies a certain disillusionment with contemporary design, which could explain why old-world clothes are back to the forefront of fashion. For more on the stars of yesteryear who are having a modern-day revival, **Designers and their Decades** provides an insight into the clothes that made a significant impact on the twentieth century. **The Art of Buying Vintage** balances this mini history lesson by presenting practical advice on how to shop for vintage, what to look for and how to distinguish between treasure and tat.

Collecting vintage fashion, as well as key pieces from today's designers has become a clever and interesting way of investing money. Auction houses, such as Christie's in London and Doyle's in New York, have taken note and hold high-profile vintage auctions annually. Contemporary designers are being inspired by the fashion archives and are taking full advantage of this obsession with nostalgia by translating long-forgotten designs into modern pieces and resurrecting dormant fashion houses. Clothes made by latter-day designers can cost an absolute fortune but, in some instances, are neither as well made nor as well priced as, say, their Forties' counterparts. Despite that, today's news is tomorrow's history so **Vintage Going Forward** features the work of contemporary designers that may have an equal level of eminence in years to come. Key pieces with investment potential are known as 'Future Collectables', so discover if it's worth paying attention to Alexander McQueen's current collection and whether it was wise to ignore Balenciaga's 2002 spring/summer line.

For those loyal devotees of costume jewellery, shoes and bags, **Vintage Accessories**, although not exhaustive, will fuel your passion further. The advice on buying, wearing and collecting accessories will likewise appeal to vintage virgins new to the world of Trifari gems and Vivier footwear.

All this information, however, serves little purpose if you have no idea where to buy the clothes and accessories described in this book. The extensive **Vintage Directory** lets you in on the fashionistas' top secrets – the best vintage sources all over the world from the hottest fair in Manhattan to the small but exquisite shop in Brighton – which alone makes this book the obligatory 'piece' no vintage enthusiast should leave home without.

Shopping for Vintage, it must be said, is not just about fashion, which Quentin Crisp famously defined as 'what you adopt when you don't know who you are'. It is about embracing your personal style in things of old and pieces you love rather than being dictated to by the current catwalk trends. So when you are out searching for your vintage gems, muse on the wise words of American writer Gail Ruben Bereny who said, 'Above all remember that the most important thing you can take anywhere is not a Gucci bag or French-cut jeans; it's an open mind'. Happy shopping.

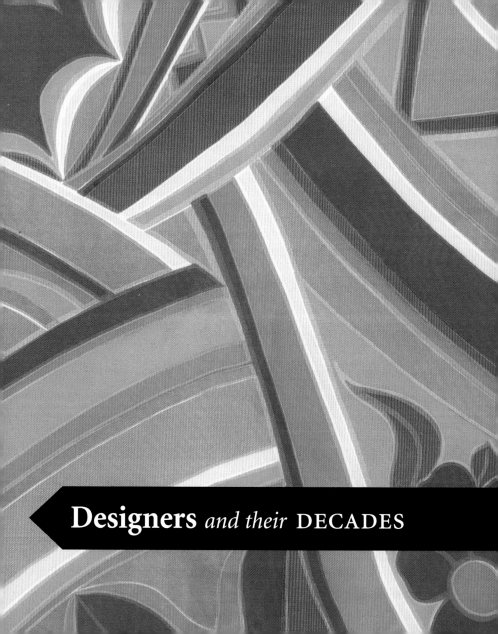

Designers *and their* DECADES

LA *belle* Époque 1890–1914

The French phrase 'La Belle Époque' refers to the pre-war 'fine period' typified by extravagant dressing and the height of luxury living for the elite. The bustle disappeared from dresses and Charles Worth's 'Princess line' – a more pared-down sophisticated version of the A-line shape – developed into the new style of skirt. Ultra voluminous dress sleeves, also known as 'Leg of Mutton' sleeves, became the norm. When these were used on evening dresses, a tiny waist and huge skirt highlighted the proportions even further. These full sleeves made it impossible to wear coats so cloaks, as an alternative form of outerwear, became very popular, particularly pelerines, which were short capes that were slightly longer at the front. *The* **S-bend health corset** *set the tone for fashionable women right up until 1905.* It was known as such because as the corset was tightly laced up, it forced the hips back and pushed the 'monobosom' forward, which created an almost pigeon-like S-shape. Tailor-made suits – first introduced by Redfern and the house of Creed – were worn with high-necked white shirts and a bustled skirt or bloomers. Although in 1880 they were initially viewed as masculine and unladylike, by 1900 they were firmly established. After 1907, the empire line and longer-line corset – almost knee-length – had become fashionable as it made women look much slimmer. Known as the 'Directoire' style, this look was pioneered by Paul Poiret.

charles WORTH—ILLUSTRATED LEFT

Who? Charles Frederick Worth was an English dressmaker who found fame in Paris and became known as 'The Father of Modern Haute Couture'.

Style and design? Opulent and incredibly expensive gowns, many of which were redolent of earlier centuries. Worth was also recognised for introducing the crinoline. This cone-shaped contraption, made up of cloth and metal, was used to support expansive petticoats/skirts and became the fashionable mode of dress, mainly through the patronage of Empress Eugenie. (Worth has been credited with pioneering 'fashion promotion'. By dressing high-profile figures in his conspicuous gowns, he successfully garnered publicity for both himself and the client.)

jeanne PAQUIN—ILLUSTRATED ON PREVIOUS PAGE

Who? When Madame Jeanne Paquin set up her Parisian *maison de couture* in 1891, it was the first fashion house to be run by a woman.

Style and design? Pioneered the use of fur as a trim or accessory. Introduced the empire-line evening dress and was regarded as the 'master' of coats.

madeleine CHERUIT

Who? Designer Madeleine Cheruit was trained in the 1880s at the couture house of Raudnitz in Paris.

Style and design? Bridged the gap between couture and ready-to-wear. Her richly ornamented dresses were a lush combination of taffeta, gauze, lamé and sequins that were favoured by aristocratic clients. By the beginning of the Twenties, however, her lavish style lost its appeal when Coco Chanel introduced simple, chic and pared-down fashion. Although Cheruit retired in 1923, her design house carried on until 1935 when Elsa Schiaparelli notoriously took over her premises.

CREED

Who? The House of Creed stemmed from a long line of English tailors (c1760) whose designs became highly sought after in nineteenth-century France.

Style and design? Understated tweeds, classical English tailoring and refined ladies suits that took their inspiration from the masculine style of World War II.

jacques DOUCET

Who? Designer Monsieur Jacques, as his society clientele used to call him, was a patron of the fine arts. Along with Paul Poiret, who worked for Doucet for a few years, he helped to revive the art of fashion illustration in France defining the role of the artist within fashion.

Style and design? The designer's opulent femininity epitomised the height of the Belle Époque. His use of pastel colours, flimsy and translucent fabrics, ornate gossamer gowns, bodices of thin ivory chamois, opera capes lined with chinchilla and high-waisted style that was the choice *du jour* before the World War I are all well documented.

REDFERN

Who? Redfern was one of the most successful English tailoring houses. It was the first to offer tailored suits for ladies that were directly influenced by their male counterparts.

Style and design? Yachting, travelling and riding suits. Created an outfit for Lillie Langtry, the mistress of the Prince of Wales, who subsequently became King Edward VII. Popularised the high-waisted Grecian style in 1908.

CALLOT *sœurs*

Who? A design collaboration made up of four sisters – Marie, Marthe, Regina and Joséphine. The Callot sisters were known as 'the backbone of the European fashion world'. Madeleine Vionnet, who early on in her career worked for the house as a seamstress, heaped further praise on the quartet by famously saying 'Without the example of Callot Sœurs, I would have continued to make Fords. It is because of them that I have been able to make Rolls-Royces.'

Style and design? Used beautiful but unusual materials, such as antique lace, rubberised gabardine and Asian silks – Orientalism was characteristic of their work. Callot Sœurs placed metallic gold and silver lamé dresses at the forefront of fashion, which became hugely popular in the 1910s and Twenties. One of the notable houses of la Belle Époque.

paul POIRET

Who? The 'Sultan of Fashion', Paul Poiret, was the couturier who turned the convention of fashion on its head, irrevocably changing the way women dress. A significant advocate of art moderne (later known as Art Deco).

Style and design? In 1909 he introduced a fluid style of dress known as 'Directoire', as they were similar to the styles of the 1800s. Skirts fell straight from the waist to within two inches of the ground and waists rose to just under the bust. These encouraged women to abandon their S-bend corsets in favour of high-fitting boned belts. He used bright colours at a time when the 'sweet pea' Edwardian colours were still very much in vogue. Inspired by the costumes of Léon Bakst's Ballets Russes in 1913, he also produced a collection of exotic designs, which included oriental harem pants, lampshade tunics and turbans – all brightly coloured and fully embellished. Poiret was famous for making trousers for women – seen as a type of liberation – and also, ironically went on to make clothes that restricted their movements. The Hobble Skirt was named as such because the narrowness of the skirt created a 'hobble effect' as women walked. A fetter – a type of bondage belt around the ankles so that only slight movements could be made – was worn in addition to the skirt in order to intensify the hobble effect.

mariano FORTUNY

Who? Spanish-born Mariano Fortuny y Madrazo initially worked as a painter before going into fashion.

Style and design? In 1907 a nostalgia for Classical Greece surfaced in fashion, art and theatre. It was during this time that Fortuny created his famous 'Delphos' dress. This was the name he gave to his long clinging sheath dresses constructed from four to five widths of silk that were sewn into a tubular shape and secured at the shoulders. These dresses, popular with actresses and dancers such as Isadora Duncan, undulated with colour, having been repeatedly immersed in varying shades of dye. The principle of this dress has resurfaced in more modern forms namely the Eighties' Please Pleats collection by Issey Miyake.

THE *roaring* TWENTIES

The Twenties revolutionised the face of fashion and is arguably the most daring decade. This stretch of years between World War I and the Great Depression are famous for the styles and fads of the 'Lost Generation', a term coined to describe a sense of moral loss. *Women openly* **smoked, drank** *and* **rebelled** *against the stiff rules that governed society right from the 1900s.* Hemlines were now at the knees. As a way of compensating for the extra flesh on show, clothes became less form fitting and brassieres bound the breasts to give a more androgynous look. The purpose of this style was to emphasise women's newly found equality with men. A new culture of sports emerged and women bought their tennis-style sweaters from men's clothing outlets. The emergence of dancing as a passion – particularly the Charleston – also impacted on the Twenties woman's wardrobe. In order to dance freely, glamorous clothing that allowed movement was necessary. Drop-waisted, slightly loose evening dresses, elaborately embellished with rhinestones, beads and sequins, became the requisite. This was known as the 'Flapper Dress'.

COCO CHANEL

Who? One of the most influential designers of the era, Coco Chanel was famously quoted as saying 'she wanted to rid women of their frills'. She saw a need for working women to wear simple, comfortable clothes that were elegant but understated.

Style and design? Introduced neutrals – beige, navy and black – in simple styles that did not require complex corsetry to manipulate the female form. Credited with transforming tweed into the iconic Chanel suit. She is less well known for creating the Little Black Dress.

jeanne LANVIN—<small>ILLUSTRATED RIGHT</small>

Who? In 1909, this ex-milliner headed the first design business to be given the prestigious accolade 'couture house'.
Style and design? Her design philosophy strayed from sumptuous, intricate beading and embroidery to sheer simplicity. These romantic designs, usually in light, clear floral colours, became the Lanvin trademark.

jean PATOU

Who? Patou launched his first collection in 1914 under the label Maison Parry. Credited with designing the first cardigan and knitted bathing suit.
Style and design? Influenced by Cubist paintings and Art Deco, simplicity with sharp geometric lines became the general characteristic of his design philosophy. Patou designed long-waisted princess-line dresses and knitted swimwear. Launched new colours every season – Patou blue, Patou green.

madeleine VIONNET—ILLUSTRATED LEFT

Who? Vionnet is credited with being the doyenne of the bias-cut. John Galliano has said he 'strives to emulate her skill' and describes her dresses as 'the ultimate in voluptuousness'. Showed her last collection in 1939.

Style and design? Dresses in draped fabrics and flowing – almost liquid – lines replaced the upholstered look of bustles and petticoats. It liberated women from the torturous confines of the corset, permitting much more graceful movement.

louise BOULANGER

Who? Louise Boulanger learnt her craft as a couturier under both Madame Cheruit and the Callot sisters.

Style and design? Elegant clothing that was cut on the bias – the back flowed down to the ankles while the front of the dress lay at the knees. Boulanger's trademarks were taffeta and bold colours and in the mid Twenties she produced the 'pouf'. This was an evening dress that, although close fitting around the torso and waist, featured an elaborate fan pleating on the hips, which gave a 'puffball' bouffant effect.

THE *depression* OF THE THIRTIES

In contrast to the euphoria of the Twenties, the Thirties were economically depressed. The 1929 Wall Street crash kickstarted this depression, the consequences of which reverberated around the world. This included unprecedented levels of unemployment, inflation and the rise of totalitarian movements. *In these troubled times,* **people found escapism in the silver screen.** Hollywood was idolised and provided a distraction from reality. This became the new medium of fashion. Clothing was simplified, moving away from the experimentalism of the Twenties. There was a dramatic drop in hemlines from knee-length to lower calf, the waist was brought back to its 'proper position', the Twenties' bob was discarded in favour of full-length more feminine hair. Underwear became comfortable and less restrictive after years of being 'bound'. Women adopted wide-legged trousers and mannish sweaters popularised by the likes of Katherine Hepburn. Later on, the wider, shoulder-padded designs cemented the image of the Thirties woman. The culture of health and fitness thrived: shorts became an essential part of women's wardrobes while swimwear became lighter and more wearable. For evening gowns, the emphasis was placed more on cut than ornamentation. Dresses were usually sleeveless – some with a low cowl neck-back – and finished off with very subtle decoration. Unlike the Twenties, hemlines were always floor-length. The latter part of the decade marked a pronounced change in style. The elegant bias-cut pioneered by Madeleine Vionnet was discarded for a Victorian-inspired look. Corseting and embellished bodices – once again – became fashionable.

jean DESSÈS—ILLUSTRATED LEFT

Who? Jean Dessès was involved in the Paris fashion doll exhibition called 'Théâtre de la Mode' which had a highly significant influence on the direction Paris fashion took after World War II. Dessès was one of the first couturiers to make the progressive move into creating a mass-produced diffusion line that was a spin off of his main collection.

Style and design? Created exquisite draped ball gowns in chiffon and mousseline, based on – in ode to his descent – early Greek and Egyptian robes. Also known for embroidered and sheath dresses with tight jackets and flowing skirts.

madame GRÈS—ILLUSTRATED ON PREVIOUS PAGE

Who? Madame Grès is the Parisian couturier noted for having a significant and historic influence on the world of French couture.

Style and design? Her designs were influenced by Minimalist art and Grecian costume – she perfected the art of draping and pleating vast amounts of cloth into a single gown. In the Thirties she opened her first house under the name Alix. The greatly admired Alix gowns eloquently captured the Classical style, which was perfected through her training in sculpture. After the war she re-established her name as Madame Grès. In an age of mass production, she insisted on haute couture. Some gowns took over 300 hours to complete.

elsa SCHIAPARELLI

Who? Hailed by the press as 'one of the rare innovators' of her day, Elsa Schiaparelli famously merged Surrealist art with high fashion by using fabrics designed by artists Salvador Dalì and Jean Cocteau.

Style and design? Her early pieces were undecorated but after 1935, opulent embroidery and outlandish accessories became her trademark. Her collaborations with Dalì, Cocteau and Paul Delvaux produced clothes that were witty and clever works of art. A hat was made in the form of a shoe, a desk suit was made with drawers for pockets, and smashed glass and mirrors were used to transform an otherwise mundane jacket into a glorious work of art. The best-known Dalì–Schiaparelli collaboration was the notorious 'Lobster Dress', which was worn by the Duchess of Windsor for a Cecil Beaton photograph in 1937. One of Schiaparelli's own noteworthy pieces was a shocking pink cape – her trademark colour – with a huge gold sunburst embroidered on the back.

lucien LELONG—<small>ILLUSTRATED RIGHT</small>

Who? Lucien Lelong was the son of two nineteenth-century couturiers, Arthur and Eleonore. Not known so much for his creative talent but gained a reputation as a shrewd and very influential businessman. From 1937 to 1947 he was President of the Chamber Syndicate de la Couture Parisienne, Haute Couture's governing body. One of the first designers to diversify into lingerie, hosiery and ready-to-wear – a line which he labelled Lucien Lelong Éditions.

Style and design? Tightly waisted, full-skirted dresses that inadvertently pre-empted Dior's famed 1947 New Look.

edward MOLYNEUX

Who? Irish designer Edward Molyneux opened a Paris-based couture house at the age of 28. He designed the wedding dress and trousseau of Princess Marina of Greece for her 1934 marriage to the Duke of Kent.

Style and design? His backless white satin gown, worn with furs thrown over the shoulders, became symbolic of the elegance of the Thirties.

MAINBOCHER—ILLUSTRATED LEFT

Who? Main Rousseau Bocher was an ex *Harpers Bazaar* and *Vogue* writer who left journalism to set up a fashion design company.

Style and design? Narrow bias-cut slip dresses in printed silks, taffeta or crepe featured heavily in his first collection. He also used traditional men's shirting fabric, towelling, gingham and cotton pique for floor-skimming evening gowns. Designed the Duchess of Windsor's wedding dress when she infamously married the abdicated King of England – Edward VIII.

hattie CARNEGIE

Who? Though Hattie Carnegie was a prominent and highly revered fashion designer in the Thirties, she had no sewing skills and henceforth never actually made a dress. Rather, she worked closely with a number of dressmakers to produce her designs.

Style and design? Developed the all American 'Carnegie look' of tailored dresses and suits, which were the simplification of European dress. Luxurious and elegant but understated with little or no elaboration. Worn by American socialites C.Z. Guest and the Duchess of Windsor.

marcel ROCHAS—<small>ILLUSTRATED LEFT</small>

Who? Although Marcel Rochas established the company in 1925, he didn't become noted until the Thirties. When the great couturier died in 1955, the perfumery side of the business flourished but, unfortunately, the couture line died with its founder. It was revived in 2002 with Belgian designer Olivier Theyskens at the helm of the house.

Style and design? His wasp-waisted Chantilly corsets heralded the curvaceous silhouette that made women provocative and extravagant. His muse, Mae West, inspired this.

nina RICCI

Who? Nina Ricci famously opened her own couture house at the relatively late age of 50.

Style and design? Understated elegant pieces – worked by draping fabric over the body, tucking, ruching and shaping to accentuate positive attributes of the client.

gilbert ADRIAN

Who? Gilbert Adrian was the foremost 'celebrity' costume designer in Hollywood. He worked at MGM film studios where he designed iconic pieces for film stars.

Style and design? Adrian's key designs were the bias-cut dress – as worn by Jean Harlow – and a tailored suit with hyperbolically wide shoulders and a strong emphasis on the waist. This was known as the 'Coat Hanger Look'.

THE FORTIES – *fashion* ON A *ration*

Seen as the bleakest decade of the twentieth century, the Forties had a hugely significant 'culture of rationing' imposed over it as a result of World War II. In Europe, the war made it difficult to import cloth and other materials from overseas and besides, the clothing manufacturers had much more critical items to make for the war effort. In Britain, each person was allowed a maximum of 66 coupons annually, which was equivalent to one complete outfit per year. In America, the 'make do and mend' campaign complemented the rigid laws put in place, which dictated the amount of cloth, buttons and trimmings that should be used for clothes. All this, inevitably, had an impact on the silhouette of the era. *Everything became pared down and* **inspired by practicality.** Women wore square shouldered military-style jackets, dresses and suits were tapered into a fitted waist and skirts were slim-cut and knee-length. Dyes were in short supply, which meant colours were muted and insipid. The occupation of Paris in 1940 also impacted on the haute couture houses. Silk was replaced by man-made Rayon as it draped similarly well and was available in a printed variation. Though rationing was still in place at the end of the war, Christian Dior's ground breaking 1947 New Look, with its curvy silhouette, was a welcome change to the militaristic clothes women were forced to wear during the occupation.

norman **HARTNELL**—ILLUSTRATED RIGHT

Who? Norman Hartnell was Queen Elizabeth II's dressmaker, designing both her wedding dress and coronation gown. He was the first couturier to be knighted in the United Kingdom.

Style and design? Known for his use of satin, tulle, embroidery and trimmings on evening gowns, tailored suits, coats and tweed pieces.

claire **McCARDELL**—ILLUSTRATED ON PREVIOUS PAGE

Who? Claire McCardell is known as the inventor of American sportswear fashion.

Style and design? Before McCardell's arrival, the Dior haute couture look – as well as imitations of it – was all that was available for women. McCardell's point was that these looks, though aesthetically pleasing were not necessarily comfortable. Her endeavour was to bridge this gap and design versatile and practical clothes for busy, everyday American women. So as a backlash to the Dior look, she originated simple easy-to-wear clothing – mix and match separates, denim fashion and pedal pushers. Her signature design is the 'Monastic', which she produced in 1938. This loose-fitting dress had large patch pockets, loose sleeves and came with a belt or sash to gather the waist. She also popularised leotards and ballet pumps. Many of McCardell's designs can be seen under the label Townley Frocks where she was the in-house designer for over seven years.

norman NORELL—ILLUSTRATED LEFT

Who? Norman Norell was one of the first American designers to have his name on a dress label.

Style and design? Under the Traina–Norell label he produced with Anthony Traina, Norell designed empire-line and chemise dresses, fur trench coats and pave sequinned capes and dresses. Norell's own trademark designs were well-proportioned suits with slick silhouettes and extravagant trims, such as fur and feathers.

vera MAXWELL

Who? Vera Maxwell was one of the key purveyors of luxury sportswear responsible for shaping the direction of American fashion.

Style and design? Introduced 'The Weekend Wardrobe', which consisted of timeless pieces using the finest silks, tweeds and wools. Signature designs included the tweed collarless Einstein jacket, classic separates and suits, print dresses, Chesterfield coats and wraparound jersey dresses.

charles JAMES—<small>ILLUSTRATED RIGHT</small>

Who? British-born designer Charles James – referred to by Cristobal Balenciaga as 'the greatest designer of them all' – had a stint in Paris working under Paul Poiret.

Style and design? Began to produce his finest designs in the Forties. In particular, 1947 was known as his most successful collection – commercially and otherwise. Spiral zips, volume, quilted satin coats, highly sculpted ball gowns in rich fabrics and his technique of draping soft fabric over a rigid structure. His customers included the legendary *Vogue* Editor Diana Vreeland and 'inventor of chic' Madame Coco Chanel.

VALENTINA

Who? Known widely by her first name only, Russian-born Valentina Sanina Schlee set up her New York-based design house in 1925.

Style and design? Oriental influences – mandarin style suits and dresses worn with obis. Her Grecian-inspired dresses were also hugely popular especially after being worn by the actress Katherine Hepburn in the film *The Philadelphia Story*.

THE FIFTIES – THE *new look*

Economies were beginning to recover from the deprivation of the war and every aspect of life was taking this opportunity to return to glamour. Christian Dior's New Look of 1947 was the phenomenon that dominated the beginning of the Fifties. After the forced constrained and downright unfeminine look of the Forties, the hourglass silhouette *à la* Marilyn Monroe and Brigette Bardot *et al*, was enthusiastically embraced. Well-fitted, tailored suits worn with wrist-length gloves, a matching bag and hat was the formal daywear look that everyone adopted. For a more relaxed attire, cotton-printed dresses and circular skirts were worn with a crinoline underskirt in order to increase their fullness. The twin set, which made its initial appearance decades ago, now returned in tactile cashmere, appliquéd with beads and other forms of embellishment. *The rise in prosperity also meant that* **socialising became de rigueur** *which consequently gave way to a demand for evening wear.* Lavishly constructed pieces – opulent fabrics and trimmings – were made in response to this. Towards the end of the Fifties, this extravagance gave way to a more casual look. The new highly informal daywear consisted of denim, pedal pushers and the ubiquitous white T-shirt. This was a foretaste of the swinging Sixties that was just around the corner.

guy LAROCHE—ILLUSTRATED RIGHT

Who? Guy Laroche was a milliner before he apprenticed under couturier Jean Dessès.

Style and design? Relaunched the use of striking colours, such as coral and turquoise. Designed pleated coats, empire-line dresses and tailored pantsuits.

christian DIOR—ILLUSTRATED ON PREVIOUS PAGE

Who? Christian Dior was the most influential designer of the Fifties.

Style and design? His famously controversial 1947 'New Look' collection – a much needed return to glamour – championed excess and opulence at a time of post-war austerity and was therefore received with both disapproval and yearning. Inspired by the nostalgia of the nineteenth-century woman, the 'New Look' was defined by generous use of luxurious fabrics, sloping shoulders, and a wasp-waisted silhouette with widely flared skirts. Yves Saint Laurent, who left to set up his own label after three years designed eight collections for the house after Dior's death in 1957.

pauline TRIGÈRE—ILLUSTRATED LEFT

Who? Pauline Trigère's name is inextricably linked with the glamorous excesses of Hollywood. Created Patricia Neal's wardrobe in *Breakfast at Tiffany's*.

Style and design? Richly embellished opera coats, well-cut day dresses, reversible coats and removable collars. She utilised precious stones and metal within her designs, and also produced collectable lines of costume jewellery, particularly in her turtle trademark. Trigère designs commanded some of the highest prices at the time because of the exquisitely expensive materials used, including real gemstones and gold.

hardy AMIES

Who? A classic Saville Row tailor, Hardy Amies was appointed the Queen's official dressmaker in 1955.

Style and design? Classically tailored suits, lower waistlines on ladies' jackets. Designed all the outfits for Stanley Kubrik's cult film *A Space Odyssey*.

jacques FATH—ILLUSTRATED LEFT

Who? Although, due to an untimely death, he isn't as well known, Jacques Fath was a respected couturier considered to be on a par with Christian Dior. Many believe that Fath – along with Lucien Lelong – anticipated the look that made Dior an overnight success. He made fashion history by being the first designer to export his designs to the United States.

Style and design? Fath always cut the fabric directly on the client. His clothes were inspired by the hourglass shape and therefore featured minuscule waists. Fath was also known for his knife-edged pleats and full skirts.

roberto CAPUCCI

Who? Roberto Capucci was a post-war designer known as the 'Givenchy of Rome'.

Style and design? Highly extravagant and sculptural pieces.

cristobal BALENCIAGA

Who? Known as 'The Master', Balenciaga was one of the twentieth-century's great couturiers.

Style and design? Sculptural designs, genius precision in his cut and an articulate draping technique inspired by the paintings of Spanish Baroque artist Francisco de Zurbarán. Balenciaga developed the fabric Gazar, which was a heavy sized silk that was both diaphanous as well as structured. This was perfect for his designs such as the kimono sleeved coat, 'balloon' and 'sack' dresses. He was bold in his use of black and brown, designed huge evening coats with dolman sleeves; full skirts bunched at the calf and the seven-eighths coat. This was also known as the 'bracelet sleeve' as it allowed the wearer to show off the said jewellery to full effect. The Spanish Renaissance heavily influenced his earlier pieces from the Thirties. His 'Infanta' gown was inspired by the costumes of the young Spanish princesses from the seventeenth-century portraits by Diego Velázquez while traditional short, heavily ornamented toreador-style jackets peppered his evening wear. Unlike many of his time, Balenciaga's career spanned over three decades. He designed clothes right up until his retirement in 1968.

hubert de GIVENCHY

Who? Hubert de Givenchy gained a wealth of experience by apprenticing under Jacques Fath, Lucien Lelong and Elsa Schiaparelli, and having Cristobal Balenciaga as his – very influential – mentor. He dressed Audrey Hepburn over a forty year period.

Style and design? His first collection was named after Bettina Graziani, Paris's top model at the time and who also doubled up as his press agent. This successful line produced the famous 'Bettina Blouse', which was a peasant-shaped blouse with an open neck and exaggerated ruffles on the sleeves. This was made out of men's shirting fabric. The Sack dress – heavily inspired by Balenciaga – and other simplistic but elegant styles were also typical of Givenchy.

THE *swinging* SIXTIES

Couture, which reigned unchallenged for decades, was deposed from its throne and replaced with young daring, street-wise fashion in the Sixties. The word Mod was used to describe the fashion movement of the decade. Originally used in reference to scooter-riding clothes-obsessed men, it was later used to denote the appearances of the youth of the time. This was a very British phenomenon. Boutiques began to emerge and the mini skirt arose out of a new sexual revolution that began with the introduction of the Pill in 1961. Other social events had an impact on fashion. When Neil Armstrong landed on the moon in 1969, Courrèges, Paco Rabanne and Pierre Cardin led the way in what was known as 'Space Age' fashion. Clothing took on an aeronautic look – shapes were very structured and colours were mainly white or silver. *Experimentation with drugs, such as LSD, inspired the* **colourful swirling psychedelic patterns** *that characterise the Sixties.* Though Emilio Pucci produced these patterns at the luxury end of the fashion spectrum, there were many mass-marketed interpretations. Pop Art and Op Art – mainly in the work of artist Bridget Riley – were key inspirations for both designers and general clothes manufacturers. Yves Saint Laurent's Mondrian shift dress is a famous example of art intertwining with fashion. Film also influenced fashion. When Faye Dunaway appeared in *Bonnie and Clyde*, berets became popular all over again. Even airlines had designers such as Balenciaga and Emilio Pucci design their stewards' uniforms. Never was fashion's foothold in society so strong.

andré COURRÈGES—ILLUSTRATED LEFT

Who? André Courrèges is known as 'Le Corbusier of Fashion'. Along with Mary Quant, he is credited with the invention of the mini. Worked under Balenciaga for ten years.

Style and design? The futuristic white and silver 'Space Age' collection of 1964 featured PVC boots, space inspired helmets, mini skirts and mini dresses. Geometric shapes in hues of white and silver became the look of the season. He was also responsible for introducing the tailored trouser into the fashion equation. The extent of his influence was proven in the fact that every mass manufacturer created their own interpretation of Courrèges' designs.

BIBA—ILLUSTRATED ON PREVIOUS PAGE

Who? Set up by Barbara Hulanicki in 1964, Biba was the most famous of the retail phenomenon known as 'The Boutique Culture'.

Style and design? No particular style. Seen as the TopShop of its day. Offered various fun, inexpensive versions of fashion typical of that era. Highly collectable.

mary QUANT

Who? Mary Quant's Kings Road boutique was at the forefront of the 'Cool Britannia' movement and boutique culture that pushed London to the forefront of Sixties' fashion. Quant, along with André Courrèges, is credited with the invention of the mini skirt.

Style and design? The aforementioned mini, skinny rib jumpers, multicolored tights, hot-pants and the daisy logo were key characteristics of the Mary Quant look.

ted LAPIDUS

Who? Ted Lapidus was a Parisian-based designer who apprenticed under Christian Dior. He presented his first own-label collection in 1963.

Style and design? Excellent cutting techniques. Produced one of the first luxury ready-to-wear menswear collections.

yves SAINT LAURENT

Who? Yves Saint Laurent was the most prolific designer of his generation during this era.

Style and design? Credited with creating 'Le Smoking' suits for women. These manly suits were worn with see-through shirts on the catwalk and inspired equal levels of delight and shock amongst the Paris fashion crowd. Saint Laurent's designs were based on a multitude of influences. The 'Africa and Saharienne' collection drew upon his North African roots – he was born in Algeria – and featured velvet knickerbockers and safari inspired shirts. Other collections featured geometrically patterned dresses inspired by Mondrian and the 'Russian peasant look' based on the movie *Dr Zhivago*.

oleg CASSINI—<small>ILLUSTRATED LEFT</small>

Who? A Paris-born count of Russian heritage, Cassini's fashion career started in 1935, when he worked briefly at his mother's dress salon. A year later, he went to New York to work under the famous Edith Head. By the Forties he was designing costumes for Hollywood Studios, dressing film stars such as Natalie Wood, Marilyn Monroe and Grace Kelly. In 1960, he was appointed official designer to the First Lady, Jacqueline Kennedy and went on to create well over 400 outfits for her.
Style and design? He used luxury fabrics to create uncomplicated geometric sheath dresses, boxy jackets and matching pillbox hats. He famously created Kennedy's leopard pelt coat and satin gown for her husband's inaugural ball in 1961 as well as the 'Camelot' look that became synonymous with well-crafted style.

lilly PULITZER

Who? As a designer, Pulitzer had a more auspicious start than most. In 1960, after eloping with the grandson of the Pulitzer Prize's Joseph Pulitzer, she opened a juice bar on Palm Beach, Florida. Her tailor made her a 'juice uniform', basically a printed cotton shift dress. These dresses garnered interest so she began to sell them at the stall and eventually opened a boutique. Her popularity reached a frenzied peak when Jackie Kennedy appeared in *Life* magazine wearing her classic shift.
Style and design? Cotton shift dresses in colourful swirly prints. Lily Pulitzer became the obligatory uniform for society women at play.

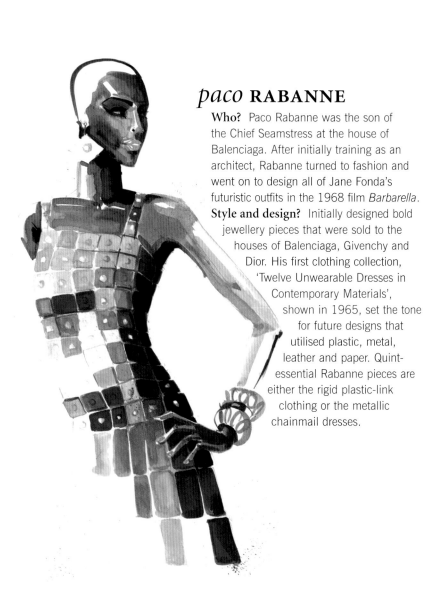

paco RABANNE

Who? Paco Rabanne was the son of the Chief Seamstress at the house of Balenciaga. After initially training as an architect, Rabanne turned to fashion and went on to design all of Jane Fonda's futuristic outfits in the 1968 film *Barbarella*.

Style and design? Initially designed bold jewellery pieces that were sold to the houses of Balenciaga, Givenchy and Dior. His first clothing collection, 'Twelve Unwearable Dresses in Contemporary Materials', shown in 1965, set the tone for future designs that utilised plastic, metal, leather and paper. Quint-essential Rabanne pieces are either the rigid plastic-link clothing or the metallic chainmail dresses.

rudi GERNREICH

Who? Rudi Gernreich was a futuristic designer influenced by the Op Art movement. A lot of his work was seen as controversial but nevertheless respected for its originality.

Style and design? He was famed for his unusual use of bright, contrasting colours and patterns. Gernreich was the first to utilise transparency and cut-outs in clothes – the topless swimsuit – worn by his favourite model/muse Peggy Moffitt – and the 'no bra' bra, were both, regarded as a symbol of sexual liberation.

emilio PUCCI

Who? Emilio 'Prince of Prints' Pucci was associated with the sporty glamour of St Tropez and Fifties and Sixties jet-set fashion. Hollywood bombshell Marilyn Monroe was a huge fan of the swirly print silk jersey dresses in fruit sherbet colours, so much so she was famously buried in her favourite green silk Pucci dress. The prints, highly influenced by the knowledge he gained as an art student, fitted in perfectly with the psychedelic movement of the late Fifties and Sixties.

Style and design? 'Palazzo Pyjamas' in non-crushable silk jersey. Psychedelic print dresses, trousers and tops also in silk jersey.

THE *hedonistic* SEVENTIES

Although there were particular style characteristics within this era – shirts had wide lapels, trousers bellbottoms and skirt lengths were either mini or maxi – *there were five very distinct areas in* **Seventies' fashion**. Bohemia comprised of patchwork skirts, prairie dresses and cheesecloth. Glam rock-inspired platforms and kaleidoscopic clothing encrusted in rhinestones. Blaixploitation featured printed kaftans, beading, fringing and anything ethnic. The obsession with disco dancing was brought on by the release of *Saturday Night Fever* so the reflective fashion was skimpy, glitzy and glamorous. Punk took customisation to another level meaning that slashed T-shirts with safety pins and leather jackets emblazoned with graffiti were not unusual sights. To counterbalance this, many designers, such as Biba and Ossie Clark, looked to the Victorian and Art Nouveau era to create a soft feminine and romantic look that was amiss in this sartorial melting pot. The majority of Seventies' clothing was produced from man-made fabrics. Nylon and polyester were therefore in their element.

MISSONI—ILLUSTRATED RIGHT

Who? Husband and wife team Ottavio and Rosita Missoni.

Style and design? Unlike other design houses who change their designs drastically to reflect the times (a key example of this is Christian Dior), Missoni's taste for zigzag patterned highly colourful knits in silk jersey have stayed consistent since becoming popular in the Seventies. Ottavio and Rosita Missoni presented their first collection in Milan in 1966. This hit the headlines as Rosita made the unprecedented move of requesting the models remove their bras so as not to ruin the line of the clothing. They unwittingly created fashion scandal as this made headlines all over the world. On one hand they were snubbed for being unconventional and on the other hand, the industry applauded them for being fashion innovators. Their clothes in the Seventies heyday of Missoni consist of sweaters, skirts, dresses and jackets all typified by the layered mismatching striped pattern.

stephen BURROWS—ILLUSTRATED ON PREVIOUS PAGE

Who? Stephen Burrows was the first African American designer to be internationally recognised.

Style and design? His designs were noted for their imaginative use of stitching. This zigzag pattern across the hemlines of skirts, sleeves and trousers created a crinkly fluted edging. This technique – known as the 'lettuce edge' – became Burrows' trademark.

ossie CLARK—ILLUSTRATED LEFT

Who? Whilst still attending the Royal Academy
of Arts, Ossie Clark started designing for Quorom,
one of London's most fashionable boutiques run by
Alice Pollack.

Style and design? Mainly chiffon printed dresses
designed in collaboration with Celia Birtwell, his
textile designer wife. Also created a range of fitted
coats, suits and jackets in wool and Harris tweed,
used an elaborate measure of appliqué and
embellishment, and promoted trousers as an essential
part of a woman's wardrobe. Created another similar
fashion line, 'Ossie Clark for Radley', which catered for
the mass-produced market.

jean MUIR

Who? Scottish born Jean Muir started her career
working as the in-house designer for Jaeger before
moving on to create her own line.

Style and design? Muir produced elegant ready-to-
wear pieces that consisted of unadorned, tailored
matte jersey womenswear. Her signature colours were
black and navy.

bill GIBB—ILLUSTRATED LEFT

Who? British designer Bill Gibb was the most famous knitwear creator of the Seventies.

Style and design? Colourful knits with intricate meandering patterns were Gibb's speciality. He collaborated with Missoni on a highly successful collection but was also known for his lavishly layered dresses, which he produced to counteract the tailored look that was in fashion at the time. Inspired by the decadence of the Renaissance Era, he used fabrics with highly decorative prints.

CHLOÉ

Who? Set up by two Parisians, Jacques Lenoir and Gaby Aghion in 1952. In 1966 Karl Lagerfeld became the house's head designer and his powerful direction led Chloé to become one of the most iconic fashion brands of the Seventies.

Style and design? Coined the term 'luxury prêt-à-porter'. Romantic, bohemian and very feminine, Chloé captured the new youthful mood of Paris and became one of the key fashion brands of the Seventies. Brigette Bardot, Maria Callas and Grace Kelly were some of the labels' illustrious enthusiasts.

thea PORTER—ILLUSTRATED RIGHT

Who? Syrian born Thea Porter introduced the
Kaftan into mainstream fashion.

Style and design? Porter specialised in luxuriously
embellished and ethnic-inspired clothing using rich
fabrics such as brocade, silk, chiffon and velvet.
Her designs underpinned the bohemian glamour
of the late Sixties and Seventies.

james GALANOS

Who? James Galanos was the first designer to
use the horseshoe neckline on his designs.

Style and design? Draped evening dresses with
billowing sleeves, sheath dresses worn under
chiffon coats and low backed wool gowns.
Galanos displayed couture-like craftsmanship,
using opulent fabrics such as velvets, brocades
and hand-painted silks.

bonnie CASHIN

Who? Bonnie Cashin, along with Claire McCardell, shares the title of Mother of American Sportswear.

Style and design? Her relaxed loose-fitting layered look, which could be discarded according to weather changes, took America by storm in the Forties. However, it is the poncho, which Cashin introduced into mainstream fashion, that the designer is most noted for as it became an archetypal piece of Seventies fashion.

bill BLASS

Who? Bill Blass helped
define the pared down
elegance that is seen as
a typical characteristic of
American fashion.

Style and design?
Blass took classic,
traditional outfits in
suiting fabrics and
injected it with a little
Thirties' glamour and
sophistication. His
evening wear was noted
for the rich luxurious
fabrics such as silks,
furs and lace.

HALSTON—ILLUSTRATED RIGHT

Who? Roy Halston Frowick – a key figure on the Seventies' Studio 54 club scene in New York – became a household name in 1962 when Jackie Kennedy wore one of his early pillbox hats to her husband's inauguration. He went on to open his own salon in 1968, which achieved terrific success throughout the next decade and counted Liza Minelli and Elizabeth Taylor amongst his clientele.

Style and design? Roman-inspired, minimal and impeccably tailored jersey dresses with a high dosage of glamour. He was also known for pioneering the use of 'Ultra Suede' fabric. Synonymous with glamorous yet non-fussy dressing, Halston epitomised the cool decadence of the Seventies.

diane von FURSTENBERG

Who? In 1975, *Newsweek* magazine labeled Diane Von Furstenberg 'the most marketable woman since Coco Chanel'.

Style and design? DVF originated the wrap dress. Jersey fabric and geometric print typify this style of dress. Usually long sleeved, it consists of a fitted top and a skirt that wraps around the body and is tied at the waist. When it first launched in 1975, it sold 5 million in that year alone.

giorgio di SANT'ANGELO

Who? Giorgio di Sant'Angelo was discovered by the venerable fashion editor Diane Vreeland when he moved from Italy to New York.

Style and design? Sant'Angelo never applied the use of zips or buttons. Instead, he worked with Lycra to devise stretchy replacements for wool and acrylic fabrics. These new fabrics were then dyed in rich colours and manipulated so they doubled up as evening tops or swimming costumes. His inspirations were vast – anything from the Seventies' gypsy to the Navaho Indian.

zandra RHODES

Who? British designer Zandra Rhodes is famous for her signature pink hair, extrovert character and outlandish style, arguably more so than her actual designs.

Style and design? The punks of London inspired her controversial 1977 collection. Highlights included exterior seams, ripped, zipped and safety pin secured see-through jersey dresses. Rhodes' later collections were made up of hand-painted silk chiffon dresses and tops.

vivienne WESTWOOD

Who? Vivienne Westwood is the eccentric British designer known for her nonconformist, anti-establishment stance. Possibly the most influential British designer of her time.

Style and design? Victorian-inspired corsets, bustle skirts, woolly royal crowns, mini kilts and cone shaped bras. The punk rock movement that she and her then-partner Malcolm McClaren were part of inspired her earlier designs.

THE *aspirational* EIGHTIES

Michael Douglas's 'Gordon Gekko' character, in the 1987 hit film *Wall Street*, summed up the characteristics of the era when he famously said 'Greed is Good'. *The Eighties symbolised the height of excess and* **celebrated ostentatiousness**. The jewelled-coloured power suit, with its gilt buttons, wide shoulders, nipped in waists and above-the-knee pencil skirt, was a sign of authority, status and sexual power. Dresses were embellished with sequins, beads and studs. Discreet labelling on clothing was almost non-existent. Designers happily – brazenly – printed their logos over clothing and accessories. With everyone aspiring for the perfect body, the fitness craze went into overdrive. Consequently this had an impact on fashion and Spandex and Lycra outfits created for aerobic workouts began to be sold – and worn – as everyday clothing.

christian LACROIX—ILLUSTRATED RIGHT

Who? Christian Lacroix is first and foremost a colourist. He is known as the man with the magic paintbrush and is credited with the revival of haute couture.

Style and design? Kaleidoscopic colours, excessive use of luxury fabrics – velvets, taffeta, brocade – and ornate embellishments are all Lacroix trademarks.

azzedine ALAÏA—ILLUSTRATED ON PREVIOUS PAGE

Who? Azzedine Alaïa was known as the King of Cling. His infamous stretchy pieces kicked off the Lycra revolution embodying the body-conscious vibe of the Eighties.

Style and design? Sexy and extremely stretchy black Lycra infused dresses, skirts and tops. In 1981, he launched his first collection under his Alaïa label that produced one of his most iconic pieces – a skintight black leather dress with zips all over it. Alaïa's clothing – an unusual combination of fabrics such as lace and leather, silk jersey and tweed – defined the 'dress to kill' era.

gianni VERSACE

Who? Gianni Versace was one of the most important designers of the Eighties. His apprenticeship began under the direction of his mother who was a couturier. He studied architecture before moving to Milan at the age of 25 to work in fashion. In 1972 his work caught the eye of Genny and Callaghan who both headhunted him to design for their individual companies. Though Versace showed his first collection in March 1978, it wasn't until his 1982 collection that he was catapulted to the forefront of the fashion press.

Style and design? Gilt, gold and glamour. These three words could sum up the house of Versace. His unashamedly flamboyant sexy dresses exuded couture-like craftsmanship qualities, but paradoxically Versace himself said they were initially inspired by prostitutes; the notoriously skimpy, acid-coloured garb that brought an almost indecent amount of attention to the contours of a woman's body. Another key Versace emblem is the signature medusa head, as well as colourful 'working girl' power suits with gilt buttons. The designer is credited with heralding the 'Supermodel' phenomenon, which created a hierarchal system in fashion by paying Naomi, Linda, Christy, Tatjana and Cindy up to £30,000 pounds to appear in his shows. Though he was tragically shot dead in 1997, his legacy is carried on through his sister Donatella who now heads up the house of Versace.

thierry MUGLER

Who? Thierry Mugler, along with Claude Montana and Azzedine Alaïa, was a key affiliate in the design trend that depicted women as Pop Art dominatrix.

Style and designs? Mugler's silhouette always favoured an exaggerated line of the Fifties' hourglass curve. They were almost cartoon-like proportions reminiscent of Jessica Rabbit. Unsurprisingly, corsetry formed a large part of his work. Despite Mugler's repertoire featuring everything from space age dresses to glamorous ball gowns, he is also remembered for his exquisitely cut suits.

jean paul GAULTIER

Who? Jean Paul Gaultier is known as the original 'enfant terrible' of fashion. Gaultier started his career working for Pierre Cardin and Jean Patou, however he rejected the finesse of haute couture learnt at these revered houses replacing it with a raw edged design sensibility that is less French and more likened to London street style.

Style and design? Happily dismantling fashion conventions, he was the first to introduce underwear as outerwear – later adapting his famous coned corsets for Madonna's 1990 Blond Ambition world tour – and in 1988 created a skirt for men.

karl LAGERFELD

Who? In 1983 Karl Lagerfeld moved from the fashion house Chloé to Chanel, where he was appointed Head Designer and Director. Lagerfeld successfully turned around the iconic French label's image, which at the time was still revered but archaic. As well as designing for Chanel, Lagerfeld launched his own label in 1984.

Style and design? Lagerfeld kept the ethos of Coco Chanel but successfully injected much needed contemporary influences. The classic Chanel suit was introduced with a mini skirt – exposing the knee was something Coco Chanel was famously opposed to – the pearl strands were revitalised with the addition of the double 'C' logo and the quilted 2.55 bag – now adapted to appeal to the younger generation – took on a must-have status. Lagerfeld has managed to turn Chanel into one of fashion's leading contemporary houses.

john GALLIANO

Who? John Galliano the avant-garde British designer now at the helm of Christian Dior. **Style and design?** His graduation collection, 'Les Incroyables' was inspired by the French Revolution. Collections that followed were also exaggeratedly influenced by historical events. Galliano's Eighties' pieces are now highly collectable.

claude MONTANA

Who? Claude Montana,
Parisian-based designer
known as the 'King of
Shoulders'.

Style and design? Strong
silhouettes with dramatic
proportions – wide, sharp
shoulders, cinched waists
and architectural tailoring.

COMME DES GARCONS

Who? The 'high priestess' of Japanese design, Rei Kawakubo is Comme des Garçons.

Style and design? As with typical Japanese sartorial philosophy, Comme des Garçons pieces are very conceptual and deconstructed whilst loosely influenced by Oriental design traditions. Kawakubo famously created 'Post Nuclear' or 'Post Atomic' chic with her 1981 collection – garments all in austere black featuring deliberate rough stitching, shredded fabric and deconstructed elements such as tops lacking a sleeve.

The ART *of* **Buying** VINTAGE

So what exactly is the definition of vintage? As a relatively new term, its meaning is open to much interpretation. Dealers haven't officially established what defines and differentiates vintage from antique, secondhand and retro. Consumers – and some dealers – use the word 'vintage' as a collective term that defines anything old. For clarification, purists would categorise 'old clothes' as the following:

Antique clothing refers to any garments that pre- date 1920 (the nineteenth century, the Belle Époque era).

Vintage is anything that dates after 1920 and up to the very early 1980s.

Retro mainly refers to Sixties' and Seventies' casual wear.

Secondhand is anything post early Eighties – not strictly 'vintage' clothing in the generic sense of the word.

If you can't remember all of the above, remember only this: anything less than a quarter of a century is NOT 'vintage'.

SHOPPING *for* **Vintage**

Even for the seasoned shopper, going hunting for vintage clothing can be something of a minefield. Knowing where to go – many a time discovered via purely accidental means or by word of mouth – and how these establishments operate – for the most part slightly different from modern retail outlets – are the first steps to a rewarding vintage shopping trip. The main sources of vintage clothing and accessories are:

traditional VINTAGE STORES

These stores sell nothing but vintage clothing and accessories. The way many of these outlets are set up can be best described as organised chaos. Clothes, bags and shoes are often all over the place, they rarely follow fashion seasons and opening times can be erratic. The reason for this is that many owners established their businesses way before modern retail practices were commonplace and vintage became fashionable. Not the best places for 'minimalists', but buying vintage from here has its benefits. The dealers tend to be very knowledgeable about the clothes. Many are not money focused and so it's acceptable to haggle. The newly opened vintage stores, however, do operate like your average high-street or designer shop in regards to merchandising, service and opening hours. Like their high-street equivalents, these stores do not take kindly to haggling. Prices and etiquette regarding discounts can also vary according to geographical area. A vintage store in the centre of Beverly Hills, Los Angeles is more likely to cater for bona fide collectors as opposed to shoppers on a bargain hunt. The prices in this sort of store will be high and, quite likely, set in stone.

charity AND *thrift* SHOPS

These stores sell donated clothes to raise money for worthy causes. Charity shops are on every high street, so, with the exception of those who live in very remote areas, they are easily accessed. Prices are ridiculously cheap and don't warrant bargaining over, especially since the money is going to a good cause. Charity/thrift shops located in affluent but obscure and less fashionable areas are most likely to produce better quality pieces at keen prices – more so than in big cities where most dealers are capitalising on the demand for vintage clothing. Though most of the stock is secondhand as opposed to vintage, if you are willing to rummage, you may discover a gem worth substantially more than you paid for it. Nowadays many charity shops have dedicated sections for vintage clothes. The staff won't necessarily know anything concerning eras, designer history and so on, but this shouldn't deter buyers. Even if you are unsure how collectable the item is and can't determine the era, if you see something you like, at those prices it's worth buying it there and then. The chances are, it won't be there when you go back. Significantly, vintage hunters – both professional and hobbyists – have long discovered the joys of shopping at charity shops so unfortunately your chances of finding a true vintage gem are getting slimmer with every passing day.

auction HOUSES

Buying vintage clothing at auctions – the major houses are Doyle in New York, Christie's and Sotheby's, both in London – is an excellent source that is sometimes overlooked. They have, somewhat unfairly, acquired a reputation for being intimidating and elitist, but this is not the case. Auctions are not just for money magnates; the average shopper frequents them also. Prices can sometimes be cheaper than buying from professional vintage dealers – particularly if the clothes are being sold in lots. Many dealers actually buy a lot of their wares from auction houses, particularly well-known designer brands. Auctioneers also tend to be highly respected specialists, so even if you are not buying, visiting the sales is a fantastic way to acquire knowledge about great clothing spanning the twentieth century and the prices they are likely to fetch. For sale dates, it's best to check the individual auction house's website as these vary widely.

car BOOT AND *garage* SALES

These are sales – traditionally made from the back of the sellers' car or garage – where you can buy, basically, other people's cast-offs. They can occur as regularly as twice a week in your area – local papers will usually carry this information. As with charity shops, car boot sales will mainly deal in secondhand goods, so finding a great vintage piece can be very hit and miss. The key to successful vintage shopping at a car boot sale is to target the older sellers, as they inevitably sell older pieces. Also, particularly in the United Kingdom, it's worth travelling far out of major cities into the countryside. Here, car boot sales are held in huge sprawling fields sometimes with over a thousand sellers who are less concerned about fashionable vintage or pieces that may be collectable. Their basic aim is to get rid of their goods, which obviously works to the buyer's advantage. Unsurprisingly, prices are rock bottom – at times cheaper than charity shops – and haggling is expected. Cash tends to be the only acceptable form of payment.

flea MARKETS

A flea market is basically a facility that rents space – whether a shop or an actual market stall – to anyone that offers used items for sale to the general public. It is very similar to a car boot sale except that most of the sellers at flea markets tend to be professionals whereas car boot sellers tend to be everyday people trying to clear out their junk and make extra money on the side. Flea markets – particularly within the United States and Europe – are fantastic outlets for vintage clothing. Prices do vary according to the 'quality' of the shop or market stall. In Paris for instance, a shop selling Leonard pieces for 400 euros rubs shoulders with a stall selling Victorian cotton tops for 20 euros. Some stores do take credit cards but cash is always the safer bet.

the INTERNET

This is a relatively new resource for vintage shoppers. There are some dealers who operate their business solely over the internet – and very successfully too. A good example of this is Enokiworld.com. The benefit of the web is that you can access pieces all over the world without ever leaving your home. Just like traditional vintage stores, prices vary greatly from one site to another. Also it is perfect for those who love vintage clothing but would rather rummage in the comfort of their home/office in front of the computer. There are a few problems with buying over the web. Individual sites are not always easy to navigate and the issue of ill quality or misrepresentation of photographs arises time and time again. Sizing however is one of the biggest drawbacks. It's very difficult to buy clothes when you can't try them on. To make matters more complicated, clothes pre-1960 do not have size labels and even if they did, they wouldn't necessarily correspond to today's sizes. This shouldn't necessarily stop you from buying over the net, they are just factors one has to take into consideration. One way to get around this is, whenever possible, to ask the dealer for measurements of the garment and see how that corresponds to your personal measurements. Surfing individual vintage websites can be overwhelming and time consuming so if you'd rather shop under one umbrella, it's worth visiting the now world famous eBay.com. This way you get access to many different dealers all over the world, as well as the non-professional seller eager to make a little extra cash. Another major benefit is that the bidding system opens up an opportunity to get a bargain.

high-street AND *department* STORES

High-street and department stores in major cities have also jumped on the bandwagon of vintage fashion. There is usually a dedicated section in the store for vintage clothes. It targets those who are either vintage shopping novices or time-strapped shoppers that prefer to shop in one location. Generally, the choice of vintage clothing tends to be small and very selected. You are more likely to find actual labels in department stores whereas the high street concentrates on 'no label' pieces at a lower price point. One thing all these stores do have in common, however, is the fact they charge a high premium on all the clothes. It is relatively more expensive to buy vintage clothes here than through the other aforementioned sources.

vintage FAIRS

Vintage fairs are a fantastic source of clothing for both the experienced vintage buyer and the newly converted. This is when hundreds of major and minor vintage dealers come together under one roof to sell their wares. This includes those dealers one wouldn't normally have direct access to. This is either because they sell only via the internet or are based abroad. Buyers usually pay a small entrance fee to access each fair. You are more likely to get the 'real deal' here (in other words, no secondhand goods). Sellers tend to be knowledgeable about their pieces and authentic vintage clothes, jewellery, books, magazines, textiles and furs are in their element. You can buy anything from seventeenth-century cloth to an early Eighties' ballgown. On one hand, it can be a little intense for a first time buyer but then it can also serve as an excellent introduction to vintage shopping as one can easily find pieces typical of every era. Prices vary and haggling is allowed. Bartering for a discount is usually more successful towards the end of the day when dealers are much more keen to sell their goods. Many fairs are every 4–6 weeks. Check individual websites for details.

Chapter 4 provides a comprehensive list of the various sources of vintage clothing across the world.

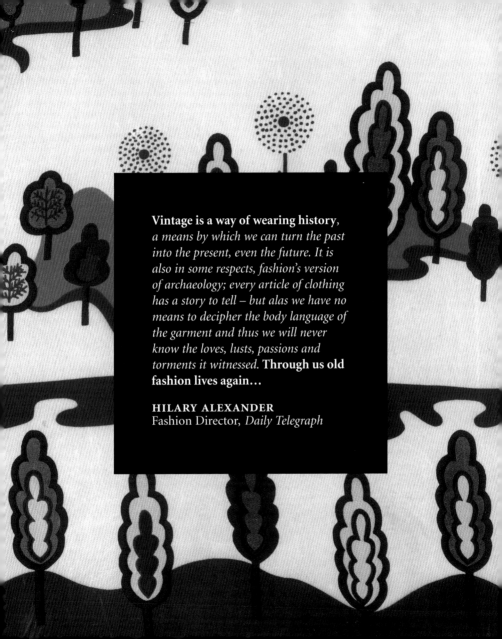

Vintage is a way of wearing history, *a means by which we can turn the past into the present, even the future. It is also in some respects, fashion's version of archaeology; every article of clothing has a story to tell – but alas we have no means to decipher the body language of the garment and thus we will never know the loves, lusts, passions and torments it witnessed.* **Through us old fashion lives again…**

HILARY ALEXANDER
Fashion Director, *Daily Telegraph*

BASIC ADVICE *to* heed...

Don't try to shop in a hurry. Most vintage stores hold a huge plethora of clothing making it impossible to root out the 'treasures' in a short space of time. Being able to pick out by just scanning rails is an art form that comes only with experience.

Whenever possible, wear clothes you can either slip in and out of quickly or ones you can slip clothes over. Many old-school vintage shops have makeshift changing rooms that are made up of nothing more than a flimsy curtain to spare your blushes. Flea markets don't usually have anywhere for you to change.

Check the returns policy of the store before you make your purchase. The majority do not offer refunds and only a handful will exchange goods.

Keep an open mind and be willing to try different things. Focusing on finding a particular style of dress similar to 'the one Natalie Wood wore in *Splendour in the Grass*' might mean you end up missing out on something that could be much more suited to you.

Be realistic. Yes, some of the most valuable pieces are found in the unlikeliest of places. However, the chances of finding a quintessential Charles James gown – or any couture creation of this calibre – at a flea market for $30 is pretty slim. Clothes that were expensive when they were made years ago will be correspondingly expensive today.

Be patient. Sometimes you may spend a whole day traipsing from shop to shop without finding the 'right' piece. When you finally find that piece with the 'It' factor, it more than makes up for the hours of sifting through never-ending racks of old clothes.

Call the traditional vintage shops before visiting. They tend to be run by local sole traders and opening hours can be a little erratic.

Try everything on before you buy it. This way you'll be able to notice any faults. Also, women's shapes have changed over the twentieth century and today's sizes do not necessarily correspond to that.

Trying on is obviously not possible when shopping on the web, so ask for as much information as possible regarding size and condition.

Not everything old is valuable.

Start with what you know. The best way to integrate vintage pieces into your wardrobe is to choose those that will work with clothes you already own. Similarly, go for styles that suit your body shape. Some are common sense. For instance, someone broad shouldered shouldn't go for a Thierry Mugler Eighties' jacket with heavy shoulder pads. Regardless of how beautiful an item of clothing is, your own taste – as opposed to that of a famous vintage purveyor – should dictate what you spend your money on. The only time this doesn't necessarily apply is when you are buying pieces solely for collecting purposes.

AGE *and* shape

The age of a garment might not seem like such an important factor when deciding whether or not to buy a piece. However, age very much determines the price of a garment. Unfortunately stories of unscrupulous dealers passing off a Seventies' imitation of a Forties' tea dress as an original are becoming all too common. There are also many inexperienced sellers who have a limited knowledge of the garments they are dealing with and therefore date them incorrectly. Such oversights can work to your benefit if you end up paying below the current market value, but if the garment has been priced up – either purposely or inadvertently – the buyer ends up losing out. The fabric, cut and style of a garment are the easiest ways to identify what era it derives from.

Grecian style dresses, although initially pioneered by Madame Grès and Madeleine Vionnet in the Thirties, became a favourite in the Seventies made up in jersey or rayon. The easiest way to know whether a dress is, say, from the Thirties rather than a very good Seventies' reproduction is to literally look at the construction of the garment. Construction methods have evolved throughout the twentieth century so look at seams and stitching methods. Slightly irregular stitching and extra fabric in the seams – to account for alterations – indicates a handmade garment possibly prior to the prevalent use of machines.

Garment fastenings are another element that can tell you a lot about the age of an item. Zip fasteners, for instance, were rarely used before the Forties. Most had hooks and eyes or were made to fit comfortably over the wearer's head.

The label – or lack of it – is also a good indication of age. Many outfits prior to the Fifties were made by dressmakers and therefore have no labels. Also fashion houses had different designers at the creative helm of the company over the years and this indicates what year the piece derives from. Over a few decades, the house of Christian Dior for instance has had Marc Bohan, Yves Saint Laurent and, more recently, John Galliano as head designer. Ossie Clark designed a diffusion line for Radley, which was made mainly in the Seventies and not the Sixties, as is sometimes assumed. A useful online pictorial resource for designers' labels can be found at vintagefashionguild.org.

Certain characteristics typified the fashions of particular decades. For instance:

—Drop-waisted dresses are quintessentially Twenties.

—Psychedelic prints on polyester and other manmade fabrics are from the Sixties.

—High-waisted full skirts are Fifties.

—Rounded collars on shirts – known as Peter Pan collars – are typically Sixties, as are empire-line dresses.

—Full-length bias-cut silk gowns were popular in the Thirties.

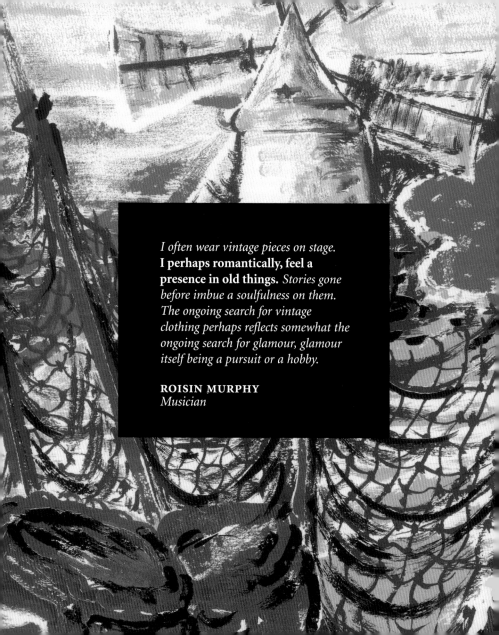

I often wear vintage pieces on stage. **I perhaps romantically, feel a presence in old things.** *Stories gone before imbue a soulfulness on them. The ongoing search for vintage clothing perhaps reflects somewhat the ongoing search for glamour, glamour itself being a pursuit or a hobby.*

ROISIN MURPHY
Musician

COLLECTING VINTAGE

When it comes to vintage, there are two types of buyer – those who buy to wear and those who buy to invest. In terms of an investment, clothing was considered the poor relation of traditional antiques. Now, however, collecting fashion is big business. All the major auction houses have taken note and have specialist departments for vintage fashion and textiles.

Professional collectors prefer to keep their identity secret. Socialites tend to be the greatest enthusiasts and, in turn, most couture pieces sold at auction are from the estate of wealthy collectors. One of the most iconic yet modern fashion aficionados was the late Tina Chow. She was a model during the Seventies and Eighties who pioneered fashion as a credible, collectable art form. She owned many great twentieth-century designer pieces. In 1993, a velvet Fortuny cape belonging to her sold for over $30,000 at Christie's in New York. Another ex-model turned collector is Tatiana Sorokka, who has an enviable collection of Cristobal Balenciaga, Jeanne Paquin, Madame Grès and early Galliano, most of which she wears. Kate Moss, Nathalie Portman and Winona Ryder are all investing their fortunes in rare pieces by Jean Dessès, Adrian and Pauline Trigère, whilst Demi Moore has collected vintage fashion since the age of 16. Although well-known figures such as Julia Roberts, Reese Witherspoon and the aforementioned Sorroka 'buy to wear', purists like Hamish Bowles, the European Editor of American *Vogue*, don't believe these couture pieces should ever be worn. Bowles has personally amassed a collection that covers the turn of the century right up to the Nineties, includes pieces from Worth, Hartnell, Vionnet, Halston and early Galliano.

Buying vintage clothing as an investment is in some ways more straightforward than buying pieces to wear. As with any investment, the purpose is that it increases in value over a period of time. To become a canny fashion collector, it's important to keep the following in mind:

Consider price If it was expensive then, it'll be expensive now and, all things being equal, will be expensive in the future. The rarer the piece, the more expensive it will be as the economics of demand and supply will always prevail. Designers, for instance, only make a handful of couture pieces; these will always appreciate in value more than something from a ready-to-wear collection regardless of how 'iconic' that collection may be. All the following points will have an impact on price.

Research your era before parting with any cash Familiarise yourself with the authentic vintage clothing by consulting an expert, visiting museums, auctions and vintage fairs.

Carefully study any labels Something that looks like a Madame Grès piece might actually be a 'Bergdorf for Madame Grès' dress. Years ago buyers from department stores could buy the license from designers to reproduce exact copies of their work. This license would include all the details relating the pattern and fabric so that even the construction would mimic that of a Grès original. One such gown recently sold in Philadelphia for $2500, considerably less than if it were an actual Grès design. A more ruthless dealer may have tried to pass this off as the real thing. Many of these same dealers steal labels from original gowns and attach them to a no-label or department-store gown in order to create interest and bump up their profits. The label of a garment is even more of an issue when designers have been known to produce diffusion lines. The price difference between an Ossie Clark and an 'Ossie Clark for Radley' is usually significant. Similarly, a designer like Halston produced 'Halston II', 'Halston III' and 'Halston IV' diffusion lines, then finally licensed his name to US chain store J.C. Penney. Look out for the white label with Halston written in black: this is the main line and therefore the most collectable, particularly the silk jersey, sequinned and of course 'Ultra Suede' pieces.

Condition, condition, condition The difference between a Paul Poiret piece in mint condition and one that has been worn to death, and has all the sweat patches to prove it, is literally thousands of dollars. Ideally, if something is bought as an investment, it should not be worn and if it is, it should be worn only very occasionally. The joys of wearing a collectable piece – especially one that is very fragile – could be cut short when you find out how much the garment has been devalued as a consequence. It is a pretty steep price to pay.

Buy a designer's most famous piece Christian Dior's 1947 'New Look' collection is always a sure bet. The year is just as important as the designer's name. The 'New Look' revolutionised the face of fashion at the time and is therefore most likely to fetch more money than something from say a run-of-the-mill 1953 collection by the same designer.

Don't buy a 'boring day dress' Regardless of how well a piece is made, Kerry Taylor of Kerry Taylor Auctions for Sotheby's strongly advises buying a designer's signature piece. 'If you are buying to collect, the pieces should ALWAYS have a wow! factor. The only things that hold their value as time goes by are the statement pieces'.

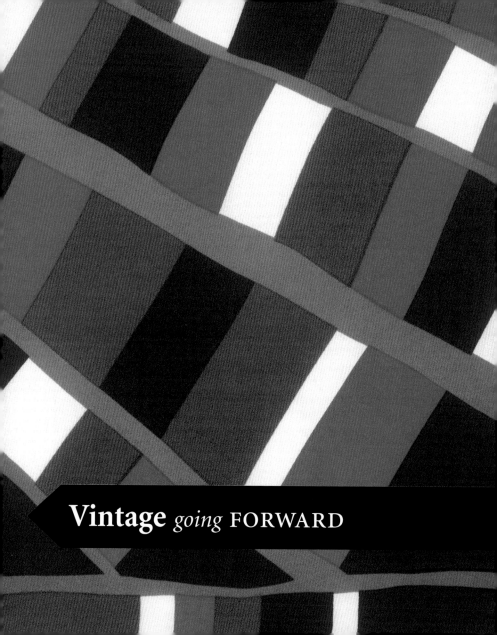

Vintage *going* FORWARD

TODAY's *designers,* TOMORROW's **Collectables**

It stands to reason that collecting today's designs for future investment is what will keep the vintage fashion business moving forward. The issue of future collectables became a hot topic recently when Tom Ford threw in the towel as Creative Director of Yves Saint Laurent and Gucci. So what should one consider when deliberating over future collectables?

Never buy ordinary pieces As mentioned on page 127, if clothes are to stand the test of time, they need either to symbolise expressively the work of the designer/era or to be simply an incredible stand-out piece.

Seek out pieces from limited collections Conversely, avoid those pieces that are 'mass-produced'. In this context, mass-produced does not necessarily relate to pieces made in their tens of thousands, it simply means general ready-to-wear collections. Also, contrary to popular belief, limited pieces do not always have to be expensive haute couture – only a handful of people can realistically afford this. For example, prices for Celia Birtwell's highly sought-after limited edition 2006 collection for TopShop didn't go over the £100 mark yet are more likely to bring in greater returns than, say, a generic pair of Prada shoes that were available in every Prada outlet across the world.

Don't over-wear or alter your purchase This may be difficult as it's always tempting to drape yourself in your favourite buy, however it's important to distinguish between pieces you 'buy to wear' and those you 'buy to collect'. Remember condition very much dictates the final price and you will get much more from your investment if the item is as close to its original state as possible.

First and last collections are good starting points The early pieces Karl Lagerfeld designed while at Chloé are still highly sought after.

Buy graduate collections from respected fashion schools Parsons School of Art in New York, Central St. Martins in England and Antwerp Royal Academy of Fine Art are a few examples of schools that have produced some of fashion's biggest designers. Follow press reports to find out which graduates are 'hotly tipped'.

Pay attention to new appointments Collections where hotshot designers are brought in to revive long-dead but august houses can prove collectable. The more reverential the house, and the longer it has been deceased, the greater its potential to become collectable. Sophia Kokosalaki's first collection for Madeleine Vionnet is a key example of this.

Consider ad campaign pieces The pieces a designer chooses to place in his or her ad campaign always inform buyers as to what he or she sees as the 'stars' of the season.

Shoot for the stars Pieces with celebrity provenance can be cash cows.

Be patient There are always exceptions to the rule, but give your future collectables 15–20 years before expecting any substantial gains.

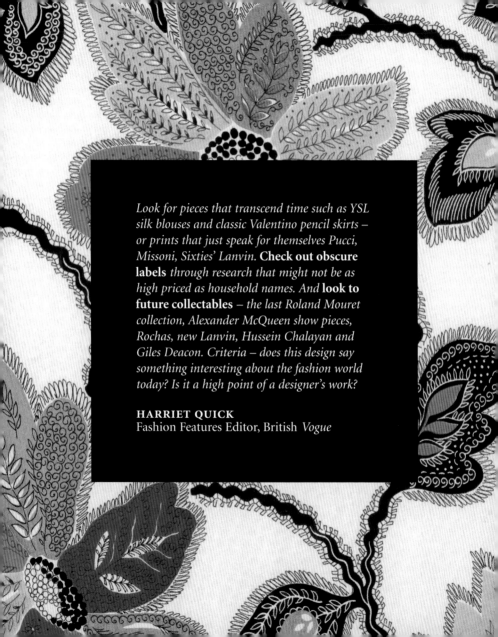

Look for pieces that transcend time such as YSL silk blouses and classic Valentino pencil skirts – or prints that just speak for themselves Pucci, Missoni, Sixties' Lanvin. **Check out obscure labels** through research that might not be as high priced as household names. And **look to future collectables** – the last Roland Mouret collection, Alexander McQueen show pieces, Rochas, new Lanvin, Hussein Chalayan and Giles Deacon. Criteria – does this design say something interesting about the fashion world today? Is it a high point of a designer's work?

HARRIET QUICK
Fashion Features Editor, British *Vogue*

KEY CONTEMPORARY DESIGNERS

alber ELBAZ FOR LANVIN

The man responsible for reawakening this august house is the current darling of the fashion world. Every collection he produces for Lanvin is greeted with awe. Elbaz is one of the few designers whose ready-to-wear line is finished off using couturier techniques. His bejewelled silk gowns have become his trademark. The risqué emerald silk dress with plummeting front (Spring/Summer 2004) is one piece to hold on to.

tom FORD FOR GUCCI AND *yves* SAINT LAURENT

The full-length leopard-print tiered coat, the wedge-heeled Oriental thigh-high boots and the dragon-print evening dress, all from Ford's 2004 final collection for YSL, should be snapped up. The Oriental theme of the collection was inspired by Yves Saint Laurent's noted Chinese collection from the Seventies. Pieces from previous Gucci collections that will increase in value include the white cut-out jersey dresses (Autumn/Winter 1996) and snakehead accessories (Spring/Summer 2004).

john GALLIANO His own line is always collectable, as is

anything from his Eighties' collections.

nicolas GHESQUIÈRE FOR BALENCIAGA His highly

acclaimed Summer 2002 collection for the house featured pieces inspired by Kasik Wong. In 2004, Ghesquière produced a capsule collection of six pieces based on Cristobal Balanciaga's collections from 1932–68. Either are great for a future collector's portfolio.

sophia **KOKOSALAKI** FOR *madeleine* **VIONNET**

Her revival of the house of Madame Vionnet will launch in 2007. This debut collection is most definitely one to watch.

alexander **McQUEEN**

His clothes are slightly subversive but beautifully crafted. Key pieces to collect are the electric chair-print skirt from his 1993 debut collection, the low-waisted 'bumsters' (1997) and the Birds of a Feather multicoloured dress (Spring/Summer 2003).

roland **MOURET**

His shock resignation in 2006 at the height of his popularity has secured his work a place in the New Collectables Hall of Fame. An obvious candidate is the Galaxy dress, however, some of the more delicate pieces from earlier in his career are also sought after.

phoebe **PHILO** FOR **CHLOE**

This French house arguably had its most successful run while Philo was its creative head between 2001 and 2006. Collect the Paddington bag, any quilted satin pieces from the Autumn/Winter 2003 collection, high-waisted trousers and butterfly necklace (Spring/Summer 2004), pleated silk chiffon halterneck dresses (Spring/Summer 2005) and white lace dress (Spring/Summer 2006).

stefano **PILATI** FOR *yves* **SAINT LAURENT**

His first collection for YSL (Spring/Summer 2005), particularly the tulip dresses – preferably in bright canary yellow – has already gathered interest.

PRADA

Although much Prada is mass-produced, there are pieces that either embody a collection or are so expensive that only a relatively small number exist. Respectively the lipstick-print skirt (Spring/Summer 2000) and the ostrich feather skirt (Spring/Summer 2005) are collectable.

stephen **SPROUSE** GRAFFITI BAGS FOR *louis* **VUITTON**

This limited collection of bags – a collaboration between Sprouse, the underground New York artist, and Louis Vuitton – is now very collectable. More so as Sprouse passed away recently. Word of warning though, there are a lot of fakes around so be aware.

olivier **THEYSKENS** FOR **ROCHAS**

The revival of Rochas under the direction of Theyskens was a revered – albeit short-lived – ready-to-wear line that employed couture-like craftsmanship. It was expensive to manufacture, which was unfortunately one of the problems that caused its demise – and not mass produced. These factors assure that the pieces will hold their value.

vivienne **WESTWOOD**

will continue to be collectable. Watch out for pieces produced in small runs.

As well as those designer listed above, consider pieces from less mainstream designers such as Hussein Chalayan, Dries van Noten, Marni and Comme des Garçons. Their collections tend to be produced in smaller batches than your average ready-to-wear designer.

The limited collections that designers create for high-street stores are worth buying. These designs may not boast the same attention to detail as mainline collections – so are unlikely to have immense longevity if worn – but in time, owning one of these pieces will carry as much kudos as an Ossie Clark for Radley. Particularly important collections are Karl Lagerfeld (November 2004), Stella McCartney (November 2005), Viktor & Rolf (November 2006) for H&M and Celia Birtwell (April 2006 and November 2006) and Kate Moss (2007) for TopShop.

Vintage ACCESSORIES

Vintage accessories serve two very useful purposes. For die-hard vintage fans, buying and wearing old-school accessories is simply an extension of their penchant for nostalgic fashions. For those who find the concept of vintage fashion intimidating, purchasing and thereby wearing vintage bags, shoes and jewellery is a less scary – and in many instances less expensive – way of incorporating individual style into a non-descript day-to-day wardrobe. A brightly coloured handmade brooch by Fifties' costume jewellery designer Miriam Haskell can give an individual twist and a hint of glamour to an otherwise mundane black dress, while for the more conservative style mavens, an old Thirties' croc leather clutch bag is not only collectable but transcends fashion and will therefore be a much-admired addition to any fashion repertoire. The old adage 'If all else fails, ACCESSORISE!' has never been more true than when considering stepping into the – sometimes complex – world of vintage style.

COSTUME *jewellery*

Costume jewellery – sometimes also known as 'cocktail jewellery' – describes jewellery that is basically fake. To put it less crudely, it is jewellery that isn't 'fine'. Costume jewellery is made to emulate that which is fine but rarely consists of precious or semi-precious stones or metals. Although it is possible to buy contemporary costume styles today, for the purpose of this chapter, costume jewellery refers to vintage pieces.

Designers such as Coco Chanel and Elsa Schiaparelli produced highly capricious pieces of jewellery that they themselves wore, inspiring others to follow suit. It wasn't until after World War II – during which there was a rationing of metals hence halting the production of fine jewellery – that costume jewellery became a dominant force in accessories. It was then seen as an acceptable alternative to fine jewellery and, once the war was over and the influence of glamorous Hollywood stars entered the consciousness of the masses, the popularity of costume jewellery rose to an unprecedented level.

The post-war heyday of costume jewellery was revived in the Eighties, when glitz, glam and gaudiness was all the rage. Once again, the stars – albeit the small screen stars of *Dallas* and *Dynasty* – were instrumental in this trend. These days, the majority of costume jewellery you will come across originates from either the Fifties or the Eighties. With that in mind, ensure you are not paying over the odds for something that is merely a latter-day copy of a rare original.

miriam HASKELL

Haskell, one of the most well-known jewellery designers –
began making high-quality costume jewellery in the
Thirties. Following on from her Art Deco predecessors,
most of her pieces were inspired by nature in the form of
flowers and animals.

Style and design In order to verify a Haskell, the most
distinctive characteristic to look out for is the interwoven
workmanship where all the decorative elements of the
piece – such as glass, beads and pearls – are hand
threaded so closely together that the base cannot be seen
between or under the elements. Other key attributes
include intricate handmade filigree detailing, unusual but
incredibly elaborate juxtaposition of very bright colours
and materials, a special antique gold plate and the use of
baroque pearls – particularly by the Fifties when the war-
imposed restrictions were no longer in place.

Hot tip Up until the Forties, none of Haskell's pieces
were signed. Inevitably, questions of authenticity will
arise. If in doubt, check with an expert.

stanley HAGLER

Stanley Hagler's extravagant designs span over three decades. He was catapulted to fame with one of this very first pieces – a simple elegant bracelet – designed for the Duchess of Windsor.

Style and design Ironically, Hagler later became much more noted for his extravagant hand-crafted designs. These were – typically – intricately hand-strung vintage beads and pearls with crystal rhinestones and coloured cabochons all set on Russian gold-plated filigrees. Despite Hagler passing away in 1996, his company remains in existence and is still producing jewellery under his name. Needless to say, the earlier designs are rarer, more expensive and in turn more collectable.

Hot tip Note that the pieces labelled 'Stanley Hagler' (as opposed to 'Stanley Hagler NYC') relate to the period between 1950 and 1983. All Hagler designs are marked so be wary if someone offers you an unsigned Hagler piece.

CORO

Although Coro came into existence in the 1900s, the height of this label's success was in the Thirties when, with nearly 3,500 staff, they were the world's largest jewellery manufacturer. Unlike many other labels, this company had a prolific output that hit every style and more importantly every price point, so the ranges were branded accordingly. Generally speaking, those pieces branded 'Coro' were good quality and targeted towards the middle and lower end of the market. 'Coro Craft' – not to be confused with Coroccraft (one word) – is the marking found on their upmarket, higher quality pieces made from more expensive materials.

Style and design Coro produced a lot of patriotic jewellery during World War II; the 'Emblem of Americas' brooch is particularly rare and, needless to say, avidly sought by collectors. They were also well known for their jelly belly figural jewellery – animal brooches with stones in the centre for the 'belly' – with Lucite/multi-coloured glass cabochons, Vendome jewellery sets and their 1931 creation of the double clip Coro Duettes. These double clips – particularly the figural Duettes featuring flowers, animals and cherubs – have become a highly collectable field in their own right. Usually made of sterling silver and decorated with colourful enamelling and crystal rhinestones, they were sometimes sold as a pin/brooch and earring set.

Hot tip Pegasus is another marking that came under the Coro umbrella, but unlike Duettes and Vendome, at the moment it is nowhere near as desirable.

TRIFARI

Trifari is probably the most prestigious costume jeweller to come out of America. It is also, arguably, the most collectable of costume jewellery brands. Although the company was established in 1910, it wasn't until the Thirties – when Trifari designed pieces for glamorous stars of the stage and screen – that it became a prominent, covetable brand. The success of Trifari was largely down to the chief designer Alfred Phillipe who was with the company from 1930 to 1968. He successfully created extremely expensive looking imitations of fine jewellery.

Style and design All Trifari jewellery is collectable but the most coveted are the Forties' Crown pins, Lucite jelly bellies and patriotic jewellery of American flags and eagles. The company had a rocky start that resulted in a number of subtle name changes and, consequently, differences in the signature on the costume jewellery pieces. The company was initially known as 'Trifari and Trifari' and these markings can be seen on their early pieces. Years later it became known simply as 'Trifari'. By 1923, when sales managers Leo Krussman and Carl Fishel joined the company, it became known as 'Trifari, Krussman and Fishel'. As a result, pieces dating after 1923 are signed 'TKF'.

Hot tip Trifari jelly belly pins have risen spectacularly in value over the last few years.

elsa SCHIAPARELLI

Elsa Schiaparelli, along with her bitter archrival Coco Chanel, inspired women to perceive costume jewellery as an essential part of their daily ensemble. Although Schiaparelli is famously remembered for her outlandish fashion designs inspired by the Surrealist art of Salvador Dalì and Jean Cocteau, her jewellery designs, though bright and bold with hints of her trademark art style, were almost conservative in comparison.

Style and design No one single look typified Schiaparelli's jewellery pieces but they were generally abstract, faunal in style using unusual brightly coloured stones and glass.

Hot tip Early French made pieces from the Forties are the most collectable. They are unsigned so it's important to check with a trustworthy dealer to establish the authenticity of any piece. Later pieces, although signed, must also be purchased with care as a large number of counterfeits were produced during the Eighties.

COCO **CHANEL**

Coco Chanel created the Little Black Dress, the ultimate two-piece tweed suit and – unknown to many – along with Elsa Schiaparelli, was the first designer to incorporate costume jewellery into her sartorial ethos, both personally and professionally. She employed the creative directorship of a number of high-profile jewellers including Verdura, Robert Goosens and Maison Gripoix who also designed for Dior in the Forties and, later on, for Yves Saint Laurent in the Eighties.

Style and design Chanel jewellery was inspired by a host of elements, including Byzantine mosaics and stained glass windows. Still popular today are her ropes of faux baroque pearls, which she herself wore by the metre. Other than those, her most desirable pieces are the Maltese Cross cuffs and brooches designed by Verdura, the floral necklace and earring sets by Maison Gripoix and the rosary-style beaded pearl necklace famously made by Robert Goosens for Chanel throughout the Sixties.

Hot tip Early Chanel jewellery in an original box is rare and therefore increases the value of the piece by approximately thirty percent. Chanel costume jewellery has been known to fetch prices at auction only normally achieved by fine jewellery.

christian DIOR

Christian Dior's opulent 1947 'New Look' was a backlash to the austerity brought on by the war years. This new look of opulence, glamour and femininity was also injected into his jewellery collection. Unlike many other fashion designers at the time, the painstaking attention to detail in his jewellery made it clear that these accessories were not a mere afterthought. They were a major, essential aspect of his collections, to be taken as equally seriously as the lavish clothes he designed.

Style and design Christian Dior had a great affinity with the French countryside. This was evident in his collections, which featured many pieces inspired by wild roses and lily of the valley flowers. Figural designs of animals were also a recurring theme.

Hot tip All Dior pieces are signed and dated. There are a number of designers who have made collections for Dior over a small period of time – Henkel and Grosse, Josette Gripoix and Kramer. In particular, Mitchell Maer pieces – designed between 1952 and 1956 – are highly sought after.

joseff of HOLLYWOOD

Eugene Joseff was a leading costume jeweller to the Hollywood film studios, hence the name. His career began in 1931, producing one-off pieces to fill a desperate need for historically accurate jewellery on the silver screen. By 1937, Joseff had developed a retail line inspired by the original pieces movie goers had seen adorning glamorous movie stars. The power and influence of Hollywood was so great that this line became a runaway success. Over the following two decades Joseff became the foremost costume jewellery designer for the Hollywood movie industry.

Style and design Most of Joseff's pieces are produced in 'parures', which conventionally defines a two-piece set that consists of a necklace and earrings. However, this set could vary to include a brooch and not a necklace or even all three pieces. As Joseff took his lead from history, inevitably his pieces were very varied in style – influenced by anything from Art Deco to astrology. The one element they all have in common is the Russian semi-matt 'gold' finish. Joseff created this visually effective gold substitute in order to eradicate the age-old problem film directors had with over reflective jewellery.

Hot tip All Joseff pieces are marked 'Joseff' or 'Joseff of Hollywood', but as with other highly sought-after labels, beware of reproductions. One of the easiest ways to tell is by scrutinising Joseff's trademark Russian gold plating. The fakes are usually a lot more polished. Olwen Forrest in Paris has an incredible collection of authentic, one-off Joseff costume jewellery, many with the matching stills of the Hollywood star wearing the actual piece on sale. Prices start from $150.

william HOBE

Like Joseff of Hollywood, William Hobe – known as the 'Jeweller of Legendary Splendour' – was a costume jeweller who mainly supplied his wares to the film and theatre industry. During a career spanning over three decades from the late Twenties onwards, he famously produced jewellery for the celebrated Ziegfeld Follies.

Style and design What set Hobe apart from his contemporaries was that he was one of a very few designers who used a great deal of semi-precious stones, such as jade and agate, within his creations. These were, and still are, therefore, much more expensive than your run-of-the-mill costume jewellery. In fact, royalty owns a large number of his pieces. He is best known for floral pins set with precious stones in the shape of large bouquets.

Hot tips In this case, a lack of a marking does not necessarily call the authenticity of a piece into question; not every original Hobe piece was signed. Again, the help of an expert will stop buyers from making a costly mistake, literally. A latter-day company bought Hobe from the original owners in the late Nineties, and while they still produce signed pieces based on old-school designs, they are, of course, nowhere near as collectable.

kenneth jay LANE

The patronage of legendary *Vogue* Editor Diane Vreeland in the mid Fifties kick-started Kenneth Jay Lane's illustrious design career. After this initial claim to fame, Lane diverted his attention to creating shoes for Christian Dior before officially setting up his costume jewellery business in 1963. His high-profile clientele included both Elizabeth Taylor and Jackie Kennedy.

Style and design Generally inspired by all things bright, bold and historical. Renaissance, Egyptian, medieval and Roman styles were all characteristic of his designs.

Hot tip Keep an eye out for his pre-Seventies collection. These are the most collectable of his range. They are marked 'K.J.L.'

OTHER NAMES TO LOOK OUT FOR:

Eisenberg Keep your eyes peeled for the Forties' figurals.

Lisner Coloured Lucite jewellery mainly produced in the Fifties. You may still find pieces in charity shops and archaic vintage stores.

Iradj Moini Originally designed pieces for Oscar de la Renta. Distinctive handmade eclectic figural designs, from insects to motorcycles, using materials such as coloured glass, crystal and bone. Signed 'Iradj'. Pieces stem mainly from the Eighties and Nineties.

Whiting & Davis The mesh spiral snake bracelets from the Sixties are particularly in demand.

Wearing vintage liberates one from the dictates of the contemporary fashion machine. *Season after season, vintage continues to influence contemporary designers' collections. The trendsetting, vintage-wearing fashionista embraces this ideology and enjoys mixing modern and old into a refreshing individual style. In a world of cookie-cutter copyists, it is vintage that sets one apart and* **creates the mystery in one's personal style.** *It is the ultimate in exclusive dressing.*

CAMERON SILVER
Decades Vintage, *Consultant, Loris Azzaro*

HANDBAGS

Whether vintage or brand new, the intimate relationship between a woman and her handbag has been well documented. Our love of handbags can be traced as far back as the fourteenth century when women decided to carry their precious items in something equally exquisite. At this point – the earliest recognition of the 'bag' as we know it – bags became a fashion requisite, adorned with jewels and/or embroidery. The more ostentatious the bag, the greater the status of the owner. By the sixteenth century bags become more practical, made out of less delicate material such as leather. Eighteenth-century fashion-savvy women started wearing handbags called reticules and owned a variety for different occasions.

The actual term handbag came into use in the early 1900s, but it wasn't until the Forties and Fifties onwards that designer label handbags became popular. Vintage bags from this period are particularly desirable simply because they are both collectible and wearable. A brand name like Hermès is more than enough to solidify their investment potential and the fabric of choice – leather – is much more hard wearing than the fragile fabrics that were utilised in handbags at the start of the twentieth century.

1920S

At the beginning of the stylish Twenties, handbags became a crucial part of a woman's attire and were designed with discreet pockets for compacts, lipstick holder, a mirror and a purse for loose change. Though the Bolide Bag – the first bag in history to feature a zipper – was highly innovative, it was the metal mesh evening bags that complemented the glamorous fashions of the era and captured the attention of the style-conscious women of the Twenties. Those designed by American company Whiting & Davis were all the rage with the high society ladies of the Twenties, so much so that designs of the said bag enjoyed a revival in the Fifties.

Key styles to look out for Metal mesh bags particularly those by Whiting and Davis (illustrated opposite), Celluloid bags, metal vanity cases (originally designed for cigarettes and change) and towards the end of the decade flat envelope beaded purses. Custom made luggage from the Twenties and Thirties are so beautifully made, they are worth purchasing simply for aesthetic reasons. They, unfortunately, do not come with today's luggage conveniences such as wheels, are very heavy and therefore totally impractical for today's travelling purposes.

Hot tip Although Whiting & Davis bags were made in the Twenties and Fifties, it's important to keep in mind that the company continued to design bags for decades afterwards. Needless to say, the earlier designs – they began producing bags in the late nineteenth century – are worth much more.

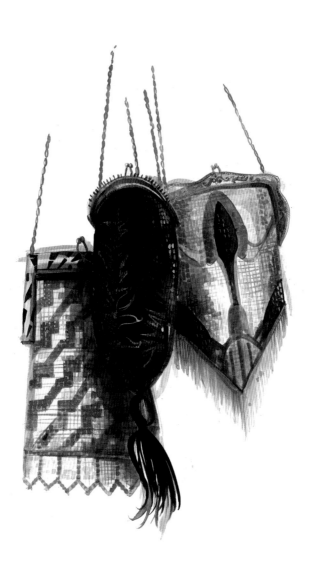

1930s

Carrying on from the Twenties, the flat envelope bag was developed further to a larger clutch-style handbag. For the daytime, these were produced in every conceivable form of leather from crocodile to snake. These became very popular in the latter part of the decade. For the evening, the bags were slightly smaller, delicate and usually adorned with elaborate beads and faux jewellery. As the decade came to an end and the Forties began, these bags grew even more rounded in shape and the fabric or leather were custom made to match shoes.

Key styles to look out for Thirties' bags are always in demand. Crocodile skin bags hold their value.

Hot tip It is still worth keeping an eye out in local car boots sales/flea markets for crocodile skin bags. There are plenty of good quality designs about even if they are not labelled.

1940s

By now, the war years had made a significant impact on the style of bags. This was the period of fashion on a ration, when governments made lots of textile cutbacks and imposed other restrictions. In contrast to the ostentatious embellishment that was so rife in the preceding eras, the coverings for bags were mainly made out of rayon – replacing silk even in clothes – plastic and cloth. The sporty-looking sabretache – a satchel-style bag worn suspended from a cavalry officer's belt – became a very popular accessory to the casual daywear dress adopted during this time. In spite of the restrictions, women were still keen to look as good as possible and continued to observe the trend of fabric and colour coordination. At the end of the decade, the 'New Look' designed by Christian Dior famously heralded a much-awaited return to glamour. This had an impact not just on clothes but also on bags. The wrist-strap and box-style bags became popular and their leather counterparts made a welcome return, albeit this time with much more fancy decorative elements such as gilt, chains and military insignias. Evening bags became very luxurious and extravagant. It was not unusual to see these bags in brocades, feathers, beading and embroidery. Needless to say, the workmanship and attention to detail meant that these precious bags were very expensive.

Key styles to look out for The evening bags of the Forties were an early indication of what was to become much more common place in the Fifties. These early examples are a little rarer and therefore collectable. The basic-looking bags that were made in response to the rationing system enforced by the war are also highly sought after, as is anything by Christian Dior.

Hot tip Alfie's Antique Market in London, Parisian flea markets and the Manhattan Vintage Fair in New York are still fantastic places to stumble across Forties' bags. If you can't get to any of these places, the internet is also worth exploring.

1950s

This was the age of elegance and the handbags of this decade most certainly reflect this. There was no such thing as a 'plain and simple bag'. Even the most basic styles were indulgent and luxurious: raffia, straw, wood and plastic bags were jazzed up with jewels, sequins, lavish embroidery and hand-painted pictures. Some were also quite eccentric in design – one style came with an interior lighting system

that enabled the woman to unearth her bag contents even in the dark. Metal mesh bags from the Twenties enjoyed a revival but most significantly, the Fifties heralded the 'designer bag'. Hermès led the way with this trend when Princess Grace Kelly appeared on the cover of *Life* using her Hermès bag – originally inspired by the traditional saddlebag – to cover up her pregnancy bump. Consequently, this bag became known as the 'Kelly' (illustrated opposite). The famous quilted Chanel 2.55 bag – named in homage to its date of conception, February 1955 – is another iconic bag from the Fifties that is still in production today. Although the 2.55 was a hallmark of Chanel's post-war renaissance it remained an icon of understated elegance until the Eighties when it metamorphosed into the ultimate status symbol for logo-obsessed fans.

Key styles to look out for Bakelite and Lucite box bags in various forms – carved and painted or embellished with jewels and glitter. Those signed 'Willardy' or 'Llewellyn' tend to be the most valuable. Chainmail bags by Whiting & Davis once again are the best of the metal mesh bags made around this time. Hermès – if you can afford it – and Chanel bags always hold their value. Kerry Taylor, auctioneer and Head of Sotheby's Fashion and Costume Department says, 'Hermès bags are very good investment pieces, particularly if you buy them at auction. This is due to the fact that the skins used are of such superior quality; it would be almost impossible to find anything on par with it today. You are likely to get more for your money by selling a Seventies' Birkin you bought at an auction than by selling a brand new Birkin you just bought yesterday.

Hot tips Always open and smell a Bakelite bag before buying it. If it has a strong acidic – almost chemical – odour, it means the bag has been stored or manufactured wrongly and will irreversibly deteriorate into a mass of fine cracks. To ensure you are not offered a plain old plastic bag on the pretence that it is Bakelite, note that Bakelite is heavier and denser than other plastics. Another sure way to ascertain the authenticity of the bag is by rubbing your finger over the plastic until some friction occurs and it becomes slightly hot. If it is Bakelite, it will have a distinctive carbolic acid smell. Many fake Chanel 2.55 bags infiltrated the market during the Eighties, so it might be worth going to a reputable dealer to buy these. Purchasing Chanel over the internet from an unknown seller is not advisable.

1960s

From the Sixties onwards there was no one particular style of bag that typified the era. The various handbag designs of the decade were inspired by whatever was influencing the fashions of the time: Pierre Cardin and André Courrèges created space age silver handbags, Mary Quant covered hard plastic bags in her daisy logo, while Emilio Pucci produced handbags in his trademark swirly psychedelic prints, which came at a premium price but were all the rage with the jet setting 'St Tropez' women of leisure. The use of black and white Op Art prints on PVC bags was rife, reflecting the dominant mod culture preoccupying the youth. In contrast to the Fifties, handbags did not carry as much significance, particularly with the younger generation. Handbags were seen as a fun, fanciful accessory as opposed to a practical and complementary addition to a woman's wardrobe. Enid Collins' bags fulfilled the demand for amusing bags by creating good quality styles – usually wooden box or bucket style – that were hand decorated with paint, sequins and rhinestones in themed designs.

Key styles to look out for Decoupage box bags – bags decorated with cut-out shapes and pictures – are always a safe bet, as are Enid Collins' ornate bags (all dated and signed), particularly if you manage to collect an entire series, such as the Zodiac range. The space age trend reflected that era's obsession with space travel making Courrèges bags a perfect representation of the decade. Pucci bags – though expensive – are is still very fashionable and is highly unlikely to decrease in value.

Hot tips eBay is still arguably the best place to pick up Enid Collins bags at great prices. Bags signed 'ec' or 'c' are much more collectable – they represent the years Enid Collins owned the company. Once it was bought out by Tandy the signature became 'C' or 'Collins of Texas' – these are not so highly sought after.

1970S

Not a big decade for the handbag, but the key style to look out for is the clutch bag in a novelty guise, such as a glossy folded fashion magazine.

1980S

The flashy Eighties was all about status symbols and Louis Vuitton, Chanel and Gucci were the key brands everyone hankered after. This can be a tricky area as the fakes that infiltrated the market probably outweigh the originals. These forgeries are still being produced even now, with some in such high quality that even some experts are fooled. Before purchasing one of these bags, it is worth checking out the workmanship and quality of the stock currently in the said designer stores simply for comparison.

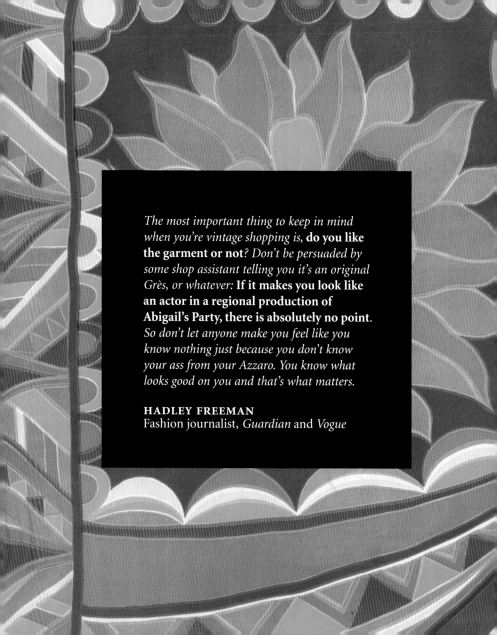

The most important thing to keep in mind when you're vintage shopping is, **do you like the garment or not?** *Don't be persuaded by some shop assistant telling you it's an original Grès, or whatever:* **If it makes you look like an actor in a regional production of Abigail's Party, there is absolutely no point.** *So don't let anyone make you feel like you know nothing just because you don't know your ass from your Azzaro. You know what looks good on you and that's what matters.*

HADLEY FREEMAN
Fashion journalist, *Guardian* and *Vogue*

SHOES

There are many women out there – including those who claim to live and breath vintage fashion – that are simply uncomfortable or downright squeamish at the thought of slipping on shoes that have already been worn to death by an unidentified stranger.

Unlike other accessories, a shoe's wearability is dictated by a woman's size. Shoe sizes ran a lot smaller years ago, so women with feet over size 5/38 or 6/39 encounter problems finding vintage shoes that fit. The older the style, the smaller and, depending on how far back you go, the more fragile the shoe.

There are, however, ways to overcome these obstacles to vintage footwear. In answer to the first problem, there is such a thing as dead stock. This refers to vintage pieces that have never been worn. Usually they are in the pristine condition they originally came in; the only thing that gives their age away is the style, workmanship and dust on the box.

Sizing is a well recognised issue. Dealers worldwide now make more of an effort to track down larger sizes for their customers, the majority of whom tend to have feet over size 5/38. It is therefore becoming easier to find larger sizes. Older styles that precede the twentieth century are way too rare and fragile to wear. For serious collectors and fashion museums, this is almost seen as sacrilege as their preservation is key. If you're interested in a style of footwear but you can't find your size, the next best thing is to go to a company such as remixvintageshoes.com, who make fantastic reproductions of vintage shoes.

salvatore FERRAGAMO

He started out making shoes for Hollywood film stars at the beginning of the Twenties, but is largely remembered for creating the wedge heel in the Thirties.

Style and design The wedge heels came in various forms but fundamentally consisted of an upper made of padded kid leather with a strap that wrapped around the ankle. The wedge was initially made with steel but the austerity of the war forced him to experiment with other materials, such as cork, straw and wood. He even substituted the leather on the shoes and straps with cellophane, which was seen as particularly innovative at this time. The rainbow platform heel is possibly his most famous design.

andré PERUGIA

Although André Perugia began trading from a shoe salon at the beginning of the twentieth century, it was only when he started to design for Paul Poiret after World War I that he gained recognition. His clients included Gloria Swanson, Rita Hayworth and Josephine Baker, while his work during the Thirties for fashion designers such as Jacques Fath and Givenchy is well documented.

Style and design Perugia famously combined materials such as snake, silk and mesh in styles that looked like three-dimensional portraits. His most well-known creation for the fashion world was probably the black suede and shocking pink platform boot for Elsa Schiaparelli that was inspired by turn-of-the-century spats – a type of shoe accessory worn in the late nineteenth and early twentieth century. As well as collaborations with fashion designers, Perugia made shoes in homage to well-known artists. His 1931 leather fish pump, overlaid with 'fish scales' was an ode to the Cubist artist Georges Braque. In 1950, his 'Homage to Picasso' floating sandal created the illusion of the wearer being suspended in mid air. His 1952 corkscrew heel shoes – inspired by his stint as a plane engineer during World War I – is still looked upon as a work of technological genius.

andrea **PFISTER**

This ex-designer for Jeanne Lanvin and Jean Patou produced amusing and very colourful shoes, which he started designing during the mid Sixties.

Style and design One of his earlier creations – a basket-weave plastic sandal in gold, known as the Deauville – is said to be the most copied shoe in the world. Other key styles include the 'Homage to Mondrian' sandals, which mimic the famous painting and the Surrealist-themed ankle boots featuring an appliquéd hand with bright red painted nails. Much later – in 1994 – he designed stacked ball heels.

roger VIVIER

Shoe designer Roger Vivier worked for Christian Dior for
ten years, between 1953 and 1963. He was known as
'the Fabergé of Footwear'.

Style and design Extravagant, highly decorated footwear
inspired by the principles of aerodynamics. Created
ingenious new heel shapes such as the stiletto and the
comma. The 1967 black patent 'Pilgrim' pump with a
gold buckle he designed for Yves Saint Laurent sold
millions. Queen Elizabeth II wore a pair of Vivier shoes to
her coronation in 1953. They were gold kidskin studded
with garnets highlighting Vivier's penchant for incredible
ornamentation. He famously integrated paraphernalia such
as pearls, ribbons, beads and feathers into his glamorous
evening wear designs.

maud FRIZON

A former model, Maud Frizon launched her first hand-made shoe collection in 1970. Brigitte Bardot, one of her famous clientele, had a penchant for her high-heeled Russian zip-less boots. Frizon did not, however, come to prominence until the late Seventies, maintaining her reputation throughout the Eighties. She designed for some of the key fashion houses of the Eighties, including Azzedine Alaïa, Claude Montana and Thierry Mugler.

Style and design Feminine and sometimes eccentric. Mainly credited with creating the cone-shaped heel in the Eighties.

manolo BLAHNIK

Blahnik is probably today's most influential shoe designer. He started designing shoes in the early Seventies and has created shoes for a long list of fashion designers that includes Ossie Clark, John Galliano at Christian Dior and Zac Posen. Thanks in part to Carrie Bradshaw, the shoe-obsessed central character of the TV series *Sex and the City*, Manolo Blahnik has become one of the handful of designers whose first name is synonymous with the ultimate shoe.

Style and design All styles are very different, however they all share a clever mix of timeless elegance and whimsy. He is said to take inspiration from a number of eclectic sources that range from Jean Cocteau films to the paintings of Velázquez.

OTHER DESIGNERS TO LOOK OUT FOR:

Steven Arpad Humorous and not particularly wearable footwear creations.

Terry de Havilland Revived the Thirties' wedge-heeled platform shoe in the Seventies. These were the most sought-after platforms of the era.

LUGGAGE

In the Twenties, an increase in travel to Europe meant ladies needed more space to carry miscellanies and accordingly required a larger purse or handbag. Vanity cases and custom-made luggage, therefore, became popular as a result of this lifestyle change brought on by the end of World War I.

Key brands The most popular brands were French labels such as Louis Vuitton (illustrated opposite), Moynat and Goyard – the oldest trunkmaker in existence – and their English counterparts Finnigan, Asprey, John Pound, Forsyth, Drew and Vickery. However, the exquisite French-made luggage sets like Vuitton *et al* are the most desirable. Goyard is particularly popular at the moment.

Collectability Although prices rise steadily, this area is not a significant collectors' field as such. They, unfortunately, do not come with today's luggage conveniences, such as wheels, and they are very heavy so consequently they are totally impractical for today's travelling purposes. The uses of vintage luggage in that respect are therefore limited. However, custom-made luggage from the Twenties and Thirties is recognised for its beautiful craftsmanship so, unsurprisingly, the bulk of pieces are purchased for aesthetic reasons. They are great as an interesting focal point within a room; many buyers put vintage trunks to practical use as occasional coffee tables.

Prices Prices for mint-condition pieces of designer luggage start from £3,000 and can rise to £25,000. Louis Vuitton luggage sets – though not necessarily practical for travelling – are the most collectable. It stands to reason that the rarer the piece and better the condition, the more you are likely to pay. Yes, they are very expensive but luckily it is quite rare to come across convincing fakes, so the chances of being totally ripped off are next to nil. Furthermore, you are unlikely to make a loss if you ever decide to sell your purchase. Good quality vintage luggage is always in demand.

Hot tip For an exquisite range of top-end mint condition luggage, head to Bentley's on Walton Street in London. Here you can find anything from a custom-made crocodile leather Vuitton piece to a Twenties vintage picnic hamper from Asprey in perfect condition. If you don't have a few thousands to spend then the best place to head is eBay.com. You will not find superior brands at low prices – if at all – but you can find stunning luggage from mid-range labels, such as Samsonite, for a couple of hundred pounds or less.

Vintage luggage evokes memories of an era when travel was glamorous, luxurious and unhurried. *Travel was for pleasure and excitement, the preserve of the wealthy who had porters to carry their luggage. As parts of the World were still relatively undiscovered, exploration was still possible. It was in this era that Louis Vuitton founded his great brand. He drew on the skills of dedicated craftsmen and produced wondrous solutions to outrageous requests – a travelling bed in a trunk for the Belgian explorer Pierre Savorgnan de Brazza, trunks to carry fresh fruit for Isma'il Pasha, the Khedive of Egypt and trunks for the Maharajah of Kashmir's polo kit.* **Luggage from this era combines extraordinary craftsmanship with exotic materials, ingenious design with exceptional detailing.** *Add to this the patina of a century and it's a powerful mix. For me, it captures the spirit of a bygone age.*

TIM BENT
Bentleys

• **Vintage** *store* DIRECTORY

Australia

—Adelaide

The Banana Room
125 Melbourne Street,
North Adelaide, SA 5006
+61 (0)8 8239 0755

—Brisbane

Goodwill Store
Merivale Street (Corner Melbourne
Street), South Brisbane, Brisbane,
QLD 4101
+61 (0)7 3844 0767

—Hobart

The Antiques Market
125–127 Elizabeth Street, Hobart,
TAS 7000
+61 (0)3 6236 9905
www.theantiquesmarket.com.au

—Melbourne

Camberwell Antique Centre
25–29 Cookson Street, Camberwell,
Melbourne, VIC 3124
+61 (0)3 9813 1260
www.camberwellantiquecentre.com

Empire Vintage
63 Cardigan Place, Albert Park,
Melbourne, VIC 3206
+61 (0)3 9682 6677
www.empirevintage.com.au

Episode
175-179 Sydney Road, Brunswick,
Melbourne, VIC 3056
+61 (0)3 9380 1777

Gigi à la Maison
307 Coventry Street, South
Melbourne, VIC 3205
+61 (0)3 9681 9889
www.gigi.com.au

Out of the Closet
237 Brunswick Street, Fitzroy,
Melbourne, VIC 3065
+61 (0)3 9419 4722

Shag
130 Chapel Street, Windsor,
Melbourne, VIC 3181
+61 (0)3 9510 8817

Speed Boy Girl
Shop 14, 430–434 Chapel Street,
South Yarra, Melbourne, VIC 3141
+61 (0)3 9826 0600

The Diva's Closet

Where? 10/11 Young Street,
Paddington, Sydney, NSW 2021
+61 (0)2 9361 6659

Why go there? One of Sydney's best kept vintage secrets; The Diva's Closet is filled with vintage finds sourced all over Australia and the US. The vintage savvy owner, Regina Evans, operates a very personalised service so you get your very own 'vintage stylist'.

What's it like? Her showroom is actually her loft apartment. Here customers can have a one-on-one shopping service while being served tea, cakes and good conversation. And this all takes place in a very boudoir-style setting heaving with the highest quality vintage clothing and accessories from the Twenties to the Seventies. European designers such as Pucci, Nina Ricci, Dior, James Galanos happily rub shoulders with their American counterparts, namely Lily Pulitzer and Norman Norell. Every item's swing ticket tells the 'story' of that particular find.

Best for? Ready-to-wear labels from the Fifties and Sixties.

Clientele? Celebrities, including Beyoncé Knowles, stylists, and the customer looking for a more personal vintage consultation. Her 'What a Diva Needs' search service also sources clothing for films and VIP clients.

Hot tip? For those based in Australia, The Diva's Closet operates a delivery service. If you are looking for something in particular, you can take advantage of the search service the store provides. This however, comes at a price, which will need to be discussed with the owner. Call before visiting – it's by appointment only.

Prices? Anything from AUS$55 for an evening bag to $15,000 for rare couture pieces.

DIRECTORY

Spunk Vintage Clothing
Shop 10, Port Phillip Arcade,
232 Flinders Street, Melbourne,
VIC 3000
+61 (0)3 9650 2465

Strangelove
221 Carlisle Street, Balaclava,
Melbourne, VIC 3183
+61 (0)3 9530 3923

—Perth

Darling Vintage Shopping
138 William Street, Perth, WA 6000
+61 (0)8 9321 1956

Divine Vintage & Design
Shop G7, 95 William Street, Perth,
WA 6000
+61 (0)8 9486 8388

Down Town Rags
45 High Street, Fremantle,
WA 6160
+61 (0)8 9336 7742

Petticoat Junction
198 Whatley Crescent, Maylands,
Perth, WA 6051
+61 (0)8 9271 9044

—Sydney

Blue Spinach
348 Liverpool Street, Darlinghurst,
Sydney, NSW 2010
+61 (0)2 9331 3904

Broadway Betty
259 Broadway, Sydney, NSW 2000
+61 (0)2 9571 9422

C's Flashback
Shop 32, 277 Crown Street, Surry
Hills, Sydney, NSW 2010
+61 (0)2 9331 7833

Cream on Crown
277 Crown Street, Surry Hills,
Sydney, NSW 2010
+61 (0)2 9331 5228

Dust 381
381–383 Liverpool Street,
Darlinghurst, Sydney, NSW 2000
+61 (0)2 9332 2854

Grandma Takes a Trip
—263 Crown Street, Surry Hills,
Sydney, NSW 2010
+61 (0)2 9356 3322
—79 Gould Street, Bondi, NSW
2026
+61 (0)2 9130 6262
www.grandmatakesatrip.com.au

Kookaburra Kiosk
112a Burton Street, Darlinghurst,
Sydney, NSW 2010
+61 (0)2 9380 5509

Melvin & Doyle
59 William Street, Paddington,
Sydney, NSW 2021
+61 (0)2 9361 4023

Mister Stinky
482 Cleveland Street, Surry Hills,
Sydney, NSW 2021
+61 (0)2 9310 7005

Pelle
90 William Street, Paddington,
Sydney, NSW 2021
+61 (0)2 9331 8100

Puf n Stuff
96 Glenayr Avenue, Shop 3, Bondi,
Sydney, NSW 2026
+61 (0)2 9130 8471

Rokit
Metcalfe Arcade, 80–84 George
Street, The Rocks, Sydney,
NSW 2000
+61 (0)2 9247 1332
www.rokit.com.au

The Vintage Clothing Shop
Shop 7, St. James Arcade,
80 Castlereagh Street, Sydney,
NSW 2000
+61 (0)2 9238 0090
www.thevintageclothingshop.com
This is one of the best-loved vintage shops in Sydney. Run by Lorraine Foster – Australia's foremost authority on vintage clothing – it has a reputation for restoring vintage finds to their former glory (known as reconditioning). Most of the pieces come from fashion collectors or older women giving their wardrobes a spring clean. Take your pick from their wonderful cast-offs – high-end ready-to-wear, antique lace, beaded cardigans, smoking jackets and Edwardian capes. Every piece is in fantastic quality and this is reflected in the price. Not overly expensive – a Sixties' beaded cardigan, for instance will cost $220 AUS – but then again not bargain-bucket cheap.

Zoo Emporium
332 Crown Street, Surry Hills,
Sydney, NSW 2021
+61 (0)2 9380 5990

Austria

—Vienna

EWA
Schadekgasse 3, 1060 Vienna
+43 (0)1 586 12 45

Flo Nostalgische Mode
Schleifmühlgasse 15a, 1040 Vienna
+43 (0)1 586 07 73

Gigi
Zedlitzgasse 11, 1010 Vienna
+43 (0)1 513 04 95
www.gigi-vintage.at

Past Perfect
Goldschlagstraße 13, 1150 Vienna
+43 (0)699 10 84 01 64
www.zeitgeist.co.at/pastperfect

Polyklamott
Hofmühlgasse 6, 1060 Vienna
+43 (0)1 969 03 37
www.polyklamott.at

Belgium

—Antwerp

Episode
Steenhouwersvest 34a, 2000
Antwerp
+32 (0)3 234 34 14
Even with a map this Antwerp vintage store takes some finding. It is just off the Nationalstraat and a stone's throw from the MOMU gallery and Dries Van Noten's standalone store, but take a wrong turning and you could end up on yet another cobbled street that looks exactly the same as the last one. Luckily when you do find Episode, you won't be disappointed. It resembles a very bright, pristine and enormous garage with pieces to suit lovers of Victoriana period clothing as well as those whose hearts belong to the Eighties skateboard culture. There are bargains to be had all over the store – a clothing rail offered an array of dresses for 20 euros or less, a huge selection of gold evening bags were on sale for 10 euros, multicoloured crocodile skin sandals were 20 euros and a mint condition black rabbit fur jacket was priced at 100 euros. Although there are some questionable pieces that are perhaps a little 'too authentic' for most people's comfort levels – such as very worn Eighties' sneakers – this is

generally a great place to find good vintage daywear and moreover a very nice and bright environment to shop.

Fish & Chips
Kammenstraat 26–38,
2000 Antwerp
+32 (0)3 227 08 24

Francis
Steenhouwersvest 14, 2000 Antwerp
+32 (0)3 288 94 33
www.francis.be

—Brussels

Ave Maria-Luisa
Chaussée de Waterloo 475,
1050 Brussels
+32 (0)2 346 95 59
www.lespetitsrien.be

Bernard Gavilan
Rue des Pierres 27, 1000 Brussels
+32 (0)2 502 01 28
www.bernardgavilan.com

Episode
Rue de la Violette 28, 1000 Brussels
+32 (0)2 513 36 53

Gabriele
Rue des Chartreux 27,
1100 Brussels
+32 (0)2 512 67 43

Galontique
Venelle Aux Quatre, Noeuds 2,
1150 Brussels
+32 (0)2 770 12 41

Idiz Bogam
Rue Antoine Dansaert 76,
1000 Brussels
+32 (0)2 512 10 32

Les Enfants d'Edouard
Avenue Louise 175–177,
1050 Brussels
+32 (0)2 640 42 45

Ramón & Valy
Rue des Teinturiers 19,
1000 Brussels
+32 (0)2 511 05 10

Timeless
Avenue Louise 142a, 1050 Brussels
+32 (0)2 648 45 52

Canada

—Calgary

Polka Dots & Moonbeams
1227 9th Avenue SE, Calgary, AB,
T2G 0T1
+1 403 262 0041

Think Twice
2133 33rd Avenue SW, Calgary, AB,
T2T 1Z7
+1 403 686 3251

—Halifax

Dressed in Time
5670 Spring Garden Road (entrance
on Brenton Street), Halifax, NS,
B2W 1K5
+1 902 463 3444

Elsie's Used Clothing
1530 Queen Street, Halifax, NS,
B3J 2H8
+1 902 425 2599

Junk & Foibles
1533 Barrington Street, Halifax, NS,
B3J 1Z4
+1 902 422 7985

Lost & Found
2383 Agricola Street, Halifax, NS,
B3K 4B8

R E Clothing
1312 Queen Street, Halifax, NS,
B3J 2H5
+1 902 422 6443

This & That
6188 Quinpool Road, Halifax, NS,
B3L 1A3
+1 902 444 7757

—Montreal

A La Deux
316 Avenue du Mont-Royal E,
Montreal, QC, H2T 1P7
+1 514 843 9893

Boutique Rétromania
820 Avenue du Mont-Royal E,
Montreal, QC, H2J 1X1
+1 514 596 2618

Boutique Rose Nanane
118 Avenue du Mont-Royal E,
Montreal, QC, H2T 1N8
H2T 1N8
+1 514 289 9833

La Malle Commode De Montréal
760-A Rue Rachel E, Montreal, QC,
H2J 2H5
+1 514 521 9494

Les Folles Alliées
365 Avenue du Mont-Royal E,
Montreal, QC, H2T 1R1
+1 514 843 4904

Rétro Ragz
171 Avenue du Mont-Royal E,
Montreal, QC, H2T 1P2
+1 514 849 6181

—Toronto

Act Two
596 Mount Pleasant Road, Toronto,
ON, M4S 2M8
+1 416 487 2486

Antiques at the St. Lawrence
92 Front Street E, St. Lawrence
Market North Building, Toronto, ON,
M5E 1C4
+1 416 350 8865
www.stlawrencemarket.com

Asylum
42 Kensington Avenue, Toronto, ON,
M5T 2J7
+1 416 595 7199

Brava
483 Queen Street W, Toronto, ON,
M5V 2A9
+1 416 504 8782

Bungalow
273 Augusta Avenue, Toronto, ON,
M5T 2M1
+1 416 598 0204
www.bungalow.to

Cabaret
672 Queen Street W, Toronto, ON,
M6J 1ES
+1 416 504 7126
www.cabaretvintage.com

Circa 40
456 Queen Street W, Toronto, ON,
M5V 2A8
+1 416 504 0880

Courage My Love
14 Kensington Avenue, Toronto, ON,
M5T 2J7
+1 416 979 1992

Divine Decadence Originals
136 Cumberland Street, Upper
Floor, Toronto, ON, M5R 1A2
+1 416 324 9759
www.divinedecadence.sites.toronto.com

Exile
20 Kensington Avenue, Toronto, ON,
M5T 2J9
+1 416 596 0827

Flashback
33 Kensington Avenue, Toronto, ON,
M5T 2J8
+1 416 598 2981

Dongtai Lu Antiques Market, Shanghai

Where? Dongtai Lu Antiques Market, Shanghai. Off Xizang Lu, which is a few blocks west of the Old City.

Why go there? It's the largest permanent antique market in China.. While the city's obsession with skyscrapers is prevalent elsewhere, this market's old-school architecture of crumbling shack-like stalls remains largely untouched. For this reason, you'll feel you've hit the REAL china.

What's it like? Stalls are crammed side by side in the meandering streets of this market. As a foreigner, expect to be accosted by traders wherever you go, but check out the plethora of antiques: jewellery, snuff bottles, Mao posters, doctors' bags and traditional Chinese fabrics.

Best for? Jade jewellery, antique luggage and glass snuff bottles.

Clientele? Varied. Chinese nationals from various parts of the country and foreign shopaholics rub shoulders at this market with one aim in mind – to find a true antique/vintage piece at a bargain price.

Hot tip? Not every thing is antique. One of the easiest ways to ascertain authenticity is to look around the market for the specific item you are interested in. If you come across a number of these, then you know you are not dealing with an original. Ultimately if you just love the 'vintage look', authenticity doesn't have to be an issue – you can make a purchase for purely aesthetic purposes. If you are more of a purist then it is essential that you do your research beforehand.

Prices? Regardless of the price, ALWAYS haggle. Prices are raised extortionately high when traders catch sight of foreigners so it is acceptable to offer just 50%–60% of the price being quoted. No matter how persuasive the trader, ALWAYS stick to your original offer -- it ensures your offer is taken seriously. Never try to haggle further when an offer has been accepted. This could cause offence.

Gadabout
1300 Queen Street E, Toronto, ON,
M4L 1C4
+1 416 463 1254
www.gadaboutvintage.com

PaperBag Princess
287 Davenport Road, Toronto,
ON, M5R 1J9
+1 416 925 2603
www.thepaperbagprincess.com

Print Fine Vintage
834 College Street, Toronto,
ON
+1 416 975 8597

Shanti
2 Kensington Avenue, Toronto,
ON
+1 416 593 0318

Stella Luna
1627 Queen Street W, Toronto,
ON, M6R 1A9
+1 416 536 7300

—Vancouver

The Barefoot Contessa
3715 Main Street, Vancouver, BC,
V5V 3N8
+1 604 879 1137
www.thebarefootcontessa.com

Burcu's Angels
2535 Main Street, Vancouver, BC
+1 604 874 9773

Kawabata-Ya
1636 Robson Street, Vancouver, BC
+1 604 806 0020

Legends Retro Fashions
4366 Main Street, Vancouver, BC
+1 604 875 0621

True Value Vintage
710 Robson Street, Vancouver, BC,
V6Z 1A1
+1 604 685 5403

Czech Republic

—Prague

Exclusive Second Hand
—Revolucní 18, Prague 1
—Belehradská 73, Prague 2

K-Oukey
—Karolíny Svetlé 10, Prague 1
+420 224 216 801
—U Radnice 6, Prague 1
+420 728 530 921

—*Soukenická 23, Prague 1*
+*420 603 863 237*
—*Politickych Venznu 21, Prague 1*
+*420 723 675 352*
www.koukey.cz

Kudy Tudy (originally known as Myrnyx Tyrnyx)
Saská, Malá Strana, Prague 1
+*420 731 163 213*

Retro
Uhelny Trh 9, Prague 1
+*420 224 215 351*

Satnik
Konvitská 13, Prague 1

Second Hand
—*Plaská 2, Mánesova 50, Prague 2*
—*Milady Horákové 32, Prague 7*
—*Rumunská 30, Prague 2*

Second Hand Market
(selling clothes by weight: for example, 1kg of coats costs 500 CZK)
Klimentská 1, Prague 1

Secondhand Ráj
Václavské námestí 27, Prague 1

Smoking Woman Italská
Italská 16, Prague 2

Start Shop Genesis
Stepanska 37, Prague 2

Toalette
—*Karolíny Svetlé 9, Prague 1*
—*Moravská 6, Prage 2*

Denmark

—Copenhagen

Ca Roule Ma Poule
7, Silkegade, DK-1113, Copenhagen K
+*45 61 27 37 60*
www.caroulemapoule.dk

Fifth Avenue
8, Larsbjørnsstræde, DK-1454, Copenhagen K
+*45 33 13 02 88*

Fisk
Krystalgade 6, DK-1192, Copenhagen K
+*45 33 15 28 01*

Glam
15, Fælledvej, DK-2200,
Copenhagen N,
+45 35 38 50 41
www.glam.dk

Kjoler
69, Nansensgade, DK-1366,
Copenhagen K
+45 28 11 13 04

KK Vintage
31c, Blågårdsgade 31c, DK-2200,
Copenhagen N
+45 33 33 85 70
www.kkvintage.dk

København K
—32b, Studiestræde, DK-1455,
Copenhagen K
+45 33 73 15 19
—4, Teglgårdstræde, DK-1452,
Copenhagen K

Kitch Bitch
30, Læderstræde, DK-1201,
Copenhagen K
+45 33 13 63 13

Kost & Mask
3, Tordenskjoldsgade, DK-1055,
Copenhagen K
+45 33 69 69 79

The Second Way
15, Studiestræde, DK-1055,
Copenhagen K
+45 33 93 99 50

Yo-Yo Second Hand Shop
31, Sankt Annæ Gade 31, DK-1416,
Copenhagen K
+45 20 46 31 81

Ymerdress
38, Nansensgade, DK01366,
Copenhagen K
+45 23 24 16 25
www.ymerdress.dk

Finland

—Helsinki

Nasta
Liisankatu 15, 00170 Helsinki
+358 40 702 7973

Penny Lane
Runeberginkatu 37, 00100 Helsinki
+358 (0)9 499 412

Play It Again Sam
Rauhankatu 2, 00170 Helsinki
+358 (0)9 628 877

DIRECTORY

Ruutu-Rouva
Fredrikinkatu 16, 00120 Helsinki
+358 (0)9 174 726

UFF Second Hand
Iso Roobertinkatu 4–6, 00120 Helsinki
+358 (0)9 603 755
www.uff.fi

—Tampere

Kaunotar ja Kulkuri
Tammelanpuistokatu 34, 33100 Tampere
+358 (0)3 223 8110
www.kaunotarjakulkuri.fi

UFF Second Hand
Hämeenkatu 9, 33100 Tampere
+358 (0)3 223 8779
www.uff.fi

France

—Aix-en-Provence

Kiloshop
22, rue Granet, 13100 Aix-en-Provence
+33 (0)4 42 96 64 62

—Lyon

Crazy Cat
52, rue Saint Jean, 69005 Lyon
+33 (0)4 78 42 69 59

Marché de la Mode
Marché de Gros, Sogley 34, rue Casimir Perier, 69297 Lyon
+33 (0)4 78 42 99 27
www.marchemodevintage.com
An annual event, organised by the students of the local fashion collage and guided by Parisian vintage fashion supremo Didier Ludot, held at the wholesale market in Lyon. Free entrance.

—Paris

Anouschka
6 Avenue Coq, 9th Arrondisement, 75006 Paris
+33 (0)1 48 74 37 00
Known as the 'design laboratory', Anouschka's 'shop' is actually set up in her apartment. Her collection of vintage clothes include pieces from the Twenties and Fifties' couture, all in exquisite condition. Prices are not cheap but then they reflect the quality of the pieces sold. A name in most contemporary designers' address book. By appointment only.

Les Nuits de Satin

Where? Marché Dauphine,
140, rue des Rosiers, 93400
Saint Ouen, +33 (0)6 09 91 32 30

Why go there? To take in striking pieces from the 1840s to the 1960s. Based in one of the famous French flea markets, this store is a must for anyone who enjoys beautiful clothes in an even more beautiful setting.

What's it like? As you enter Marché Dauphine, the first thing you see are exquisitely dressed models along the balustrade. This open-plan store straddles both sides of the Marché, linked by a balcony; the space is an absolute joy to shop in. On the Sixties' side of the store, the décor is exquisite – modern wooden floors are juxtaposed with Rococo picture frames housing vintage lingerie, an extensive collection of mint condition hats, a glass case crammed full of delicate sequinned fabrics, elaborately beaded bags and rows of wildly printed dresses, skirts and more mannequins adorned with glamorous frocks. The 1900s' section is dedicated to Victoriana. You'll find lingerie you never even knew existed.

Best for? Corsets that will give you the waist you've always dreamt of, frou-frou petticoats, mint condition Leonard dresses, Chloé pieces, statement-making but wearable hats, beautiful silk chiffon dresses…

Clientele? Collectors of vintage lingerie. The selection of undergarments is extensive, Les Nuits de Satin have been known to show them at exhibitions in Parisian art galleries. The store is frequented by anyone looking for 'the dress'. Here you are almost guaranteed to discover it.

Hot tip? Remember that this place only opens from Friday to Monday as it is part of the flea market. Also, set your budget before you arrive. With so much choice, it is very easy to overspend.

Prices? A silk chiffon hand-painted skirt with silver thread details costs 60 euros, a 1925 silk chiffon hand-beaded split sleeve dress is 480 euros and a Duchess satin Oscar-worthy dress is 250 euros.

DIRECTORY

Artémise & Cunégonde
Marché Serpette, Stand 28, Alle 1,
110, rue des Rosiers, 93400
Saint Ouen
+33 (0)1 40 10 02 21
www.artemise.net-assembly.com
This small stand in the Serpette flea market is run by friendly mother and daughter team Monique and Clara Larde. They specialise in clothes from 1880–1970. Key pieces include a heavily sequinned Thirties' gown priced at 3000 euros, a floral 1952 Dior cocktail dress was 5000 euros and a range of Chanel jewellery made by Gripoix started at 1500 euros. Not cheap but the pieces are of exceptional calibre.

Catherine Arigoni
14, rue de Beaune, 75007 Paris
+33 (0)1 42 60 50 99

Come on Eileen
16–18, rue des Taillandiers,
75011 Paris
+33 (0)1 43 38 12 11

Didier Ludot
20–24, galerie de Montpensier,
Jardin du Palais Royal, 75001 Paris
+33 (0)1 42 96 06 56
www.didierludot.com
Arguably the best and most prestigious vintage shop in France. Stocks the most exquisite haute couture pieces from Chanel, Molyneux, Courreges, Grès, Jean Desses, Jacques Fath, Schiaparelli... the list goes on and on. Also has concessions in Harrods in London, Printemps in Paris and Barney's New York. Only for serious buyers – the prices are exorbitant. By appointment only.

Guerrisold
17, bis boulevard Rochechouart,
75009 Paris
+33 (0)1 45 26 13 12
Features rack upon rack of clothes from the Sixties to the Seventies. Great for everyday vintage wear at affordable prices, which start from 10 euros.

Iglaine
12, rue de la Grande Truanderie,
75001 Paris
+33 (0)1 42 36 19 91

Kiliwatch
64, rue Tiquetonne, 75002 Paris
+33 (0)1 42 21 17 37
www.kiliwatch.net

La Belle Epoque
10, rue de Poitou, 75003 Paris
+33 (0)1 6 80 77 71 32

Les Marches de Catherine B
1, rue Guisarde, 75006 Paris
+33 (0)1 43 54 74 18
www.catherine-b.com

Olwen Forest
Marché Serpette, Stands 5 & 7,
Allée 3, 110, rue des Rosiers,
93400 Saint Ouen
+33 (0)1 40 11 96 38
Any jewellery fan visiting this outer Parisian flea market must make a special effort to stop at this store. Forest is a first-class dealer and owner of one of the world's most extensive collections of vintage jewellery. Rare pieces on show include original gems worn by the likes of Elizabeth Taylor in *Cleopatra* and statement pieces from Schiaparelli – mostly from the Thirties – Miriam Haskell, Balenciaga, Josef of Hollywood and Chanel. A must-see. Prices start from 150 euros.

Quidam de Revel
24–26, rue de Poitou, 75003 Paris
+33 (0)1 42 71 37 07
www.quidam-de-revel.com

Terrain Vogue
13, rue Keller, 75011 Paris
+33 (0)1 43 14 03 23

Germany

—Berlin

Allerlei Schönes
Begonienplatz 3, 12203 Berlin
+49 (0)30 80 49 61 38
www.allerlei-schoenes-berlin.de

Almuth Schulz
Prinzessinnenstraße 2, 12307 Berlin
+49 (0)30 76 40 41 02

Amorim Nonia Rahalho
Hobrechtstraße 14, 12047 Berlin
+49 (0)30 81 86 03 58

Ariane
Mommsenstraße 4, 10629 Berlin
+49 (0)30 881 74 36

Artemoda 1st & 2nd hand
Leonhardstraße 5, 14057 Berlin,
+49 (0)30 324 88 57

Assad
Brunnenstraße 111b, 13355 Berlin
+49 (0)30 46 30 97 74

Bärchen
Goethestraße 48, 10625 Berlin
+49 (0)30 312 67 03

DIRECTORY

The whole vintage movement is about individuality, 'What have I got and what can I wear that no-one else has?' This is a good thing because it signals the end – for the time being at least – of the costly concept of 'matchy-matchy'. Even Americans are into vintage (read second-hand) and when they have finally cast aside the idea of wearing co-ordinating colours and fabrics, you know something is up. **The vintage movement has opened up the fashion spectrum from couture to high street** *– there are far greater possibilities now for designers and customers. Very little is off limits, experimentation is encouraged.* **At the end of the day wearing what works for you rather than what comes down the runway is really what fashion is all about.** *That fashion is so much more open minded now, is due in no small part to the vintage movement. Collectables: Tom Ford's black velvet ruffled smoking jacket (I kick myself periodically for not buying it), early Marni suede jackets, Azzedine bodies, anything from Matthew Williamson's very first Electric Angels collection, early Prada sport, Isaac Mizrahi early Nineties jackets, Westwood pirate prints. Future collectables: Roland Mouret dresses, Christopher Bailey for Burberry Prorsum cropped jackets and Lanvin.*

TINA GAUDOIN
Style Director, *The Times*

Barisa Mode Second-Hand Boutique
Suarezstraße 62, 14057 Berlin
+49 (0)30 32 30 32 85

Betina Teetzmann
Leonhardtstraße 11, 14057 Berlin
+49 (0)30 32 30 35 02

Bolero
Leibnizstraße 44, 10629 Berlin
+49 (0)30 31 80 80 70

Bonbon's
Albrechtstraße 110, 12167 Berlin
+49 (0)30 79 70 04 86

Brown's First & Secondhand
Homburger Straße 2, 14197 Berlin
+49 (0)30 821 80 22

Bullerbü Kinder-Secondhand
Machnower Straße 7a, 14165 Berlin
+49 (0)30 84 72 38 76

Calypso
Münzstraße 16, 10178 Berlin
+49 (0)30 281 61 65

Caro
Mommsenstraße 65, 10629 Berlin
+49 (0)30 88 62 42 00

Chanis
Damaschkestraße 4, 10711 Berlin
+49 (0)30 31 00 42 57

Checkpoint
Mehringdamm 57, 10715 Berlin
+49 (0)30 694 43 44

Clarabella Chic Und Antik
Gabriel-Max Straße 21, 10245 Berlin
+49 (0)30 66 76 32 52

Colours
1st courtyard, Bergmannstraße 102,
10961 Berlin
+49 (0)30 694 33 48

Colpeppers
Rheinstraße 61, 12159 Berlin
+49 (0)30 85 07 32 05

Copperfire
Güntzelstraße 38, 10717 Berlin
+49 (0)30 86 39 90 33

Detlef Wiehr
Senftenberger Ring 44g, 13435
Berlin
+49 (0)30 416 67 35

Dorn-Röschen
Schönhauser Allee 64, 10437 Berlin
+49 (0)30 47 08 07 31

Dralon
Danziger Straße 45, 10435 Berlin
+49 (0)30 440 85 58

DIRECTORY

Efamilia
Schillerstraße 35, 10627 Berlin
+49 (0)30 31 80 20 21

Emad Salama
Langhansstraße 102, 13086 Berlin
+49 (0)30 92 37 27 61

Eno Wohlgemuth
Schlesische Straße 31, 10997
Berlin
+49 (0)30 61 28 56 88

Faster Pussycat!
Mehringdamm 55, 10961 Berlin
+49 (30) 69 50 66 00

FirstSecond
Goltzstraße 13, 10781 Berlin
+49 (0)30 216 55 88

Froschkönigin
Senefelderstraße 1, 10437 Berlin
+49 (0)30 44 04 37 71

Garage
Ahornstraÿe 2, 10787 Berlin
+49 (0)30 211 27 60
One of Berlin's biggest vintage shops, Garage stands out from the rest as it sells all clothes according to weight. At 14 euros per kilo you can buy vintage jeans, Fifties' debutante-style frocks, Sixties' blouses and extrovert fashions

from the Eighties. You won't find haute couture pieces within the enormous selection of clothing. What you will come across are retro clothes you can integrate into your normal wardrobe.

Gudrun Hörr
Mehringdamm 25, 10961 Berlin
+49 (0)30 694 77 35

Heidi Pacher
Am Juliusturm 44, 13599 Berlin
+40 (0)30 35 40 56 15

Heike Orth
Richardstraße 110, 12043 Berlin
+49 (0)30 68 08 71 37

Humana
Karl-Liebknecht-Straße 30, 10243
Berlin
+49 (0)30 242 30 00

Humana Second-Hand-Kleidung
Schönhauser Allee 90, 10439 Berlin
+49 (0)30 447 91 50

Ina Beditsch
Bahnhofstraße 40, 14959 Trebbin
+49 (0)337 311 25 16

Krümelchen
Koblenzer Straße 1, 10715 Berlin
+49 (0)30 853 10 24

La Bottega
Akazienstraße 7, 10823 Berlin
+49 (0)30 781 67 17

Lindt
Körtestraße 16, 10967 Berlin
+49 (0)30 691 79 10

Macy's
Mommsenstraße 2, 10629 Berlin
+49 (0)30 881 13 63

Made in Berlin
Potsdamer Straße 106, 10785 Berlin
+49 (0)30 262 24 31

Manuela Mum-Kieper
Sybelstraße 47, 10629 Berlin
+49 (0)30 32 70 87 42

Marianne Lucas
Wilhelmsaue 133, 10715 Berlin
+49 (0)30 86 42 03 93

Mäuseparadies
Halskestraße 33, 12167 Berlin
+49 (0)30 79 78 34 63

Menzel & Menzel
Fasanenstraße 41, 10719 Berlin
+49 (0)30 854 35 00

Mezzo Secondhand
Nehringstraße 2, 14059 Berlin
+49 (0)30 32 10 37 10

MOFU Mona's Fundgrube
Hauptstraße 61a, 15378 Herzfelde
+49 (0)3343 48 05 04

Paris Second Hand
Rigaer Straße 41, 10247 Berlin
+49 (0)30 49 85 44 85

Paul's Boutique
Oderberger Straße 47, 10435 Berlin
+49 (0)30 44 03 37 37

Querschnitt
Droysenstraße 13, 10629 Berlin
+49 (0)30 324 37 45

Red Star
Kastanienallee 87, 10435 Berlin
+49 (0)30 44 04 89 55

Schatzinsel
Garnstraße 12, 14482 Potsdam
+49 (0)331 201 76 24

Schnullerpiraten
Ortolfstraße 208, 12524 Berlin
+49 (0)30 67 80 17 00

Schumann's Company
Danziger Straße 48, 10435 Berlin
+49 (0)30 441 59 50
www.schumanns-company.com

197

DIRECTORY

Schnick dee Second-Hand &
Kostümverleih
Gotenstraße 73, 10829 Berlin
+49 (0)30 81 82 83 22

Second Hand Frauenzimmer
Eisenacher Straße 49, 10823 Berlin
+49 (0)30 78 71 95 00

Second Hand Laden Anna
Südwestkorso 20, 14197 Berlin
+49 (0)30 82 70 43 44

Second Hand Moderna
Viktoria-Luise-Platz 7, 10777 Berlin
+49 (0)30 86 39 30 52

Second Hand Partenheimer
*Wilmersdorfer Straße 68, 10629
Berlin*
+49 (0)30 32 76 51 22

Second Hand Treff Dana
Scherenbergstr. 8a, 10439 Berlin
+49 (0)30 54 71 47 97

Second Hand Viktor & Luise
Welserstraße 10–12, 10777 Berlin
+40 (0)30 21 23 57 70

Second'o
Mommsenstraße 61, 10629 Berlin
+49 (0)30 881 22 91

Secondella
Konstanzer Straße 57, 10707 Berlin
+49 (0)30 69 50 80 31

Sentimental Journey
Husemannstraße 5, 10435 Berlin
+49 (0)30 44 32 86 64

Sgt Peppers
Kastanienallee 91–92, 10435 Berlin
+49 (0)30 448 11 21

Silhouette i Farbenreigen
Belziger Straße 19, 10823 Berlin
+49 (0)30 78 71 20 38

Spatenstich Textil
Danziger Straße 10, Prenzlauer Berg
+49 (0)30 62 84 30 09

Sterling Gold
Oranienburger Straße 32, Berlin
+49 (0)30 28 09 65 00/2
Sterling Gold owner Michael Boenke
has turned his own personal collection
of vintage clothes into a thriving
business. This store showcases a
selection of the 250,000 strong
dresses he has amassed over a period
of 20 years. These dresses – from the
Forties to Eighties – are incredibly well
preserved and arranged in store by
colour. A dressmaker is also on hand to
redesign the dress so it fits perfectly.

Stöberstübchen
Gartenfelder Straße 84, 13599 Berlin
+49 (0)30 33 50 39 28

Stube
Scharnweberstraße 48a, 13405 Berlin
+49 (0)30 28 03 93 89

Sylvia Keil
Raumerstraße 35, 10437 Berlin
+49 (0)30 447 66 02

Tenderloin
Alte Schönhauser Straße 30, 10119
Berlin
+49 (0)30 42 01 57 85

Tragbar
Hufelandstraße 25, 10407 Berlin
+49 (030) 48 62 45 11
www.tragbar-berlin.de

Tragfläche Fries & Winter
Pappelallee 10, 10437 Berlin
+49 (0)30 49 85 32 75

Trechic Second-Hand
Wühlischstraße 31, 10245 Berlin
+49 (0)30 27 57 44 35

Treibstoff
Bergmannstraße 106, 10961 Berlin
+49 (0)30 693 82 99

Trippel Trappel
Schönfließer Straße 19, 16540
Hohen Neuendorf
+40 (0)3303 21 73 72

Waahnsinn Berlin
Rosenthaler Straße 17, 10119 Berlin
+49 (0)30 282 00 29
www.waahnsinn-berlin.de

Zohra Hill
Husemannstraße 16, 10435 Berlin
+49 (0)30 442 44 73

—Cologne

Entlarvt
Zülpicher Straße 6, Uni-Viertel,
50674 Cologne
+49 (0)221 240 68 10

Kaufhaus Kilo
Ehrenstraße 28, Innenstadt,
50672 Cologne
+49 (0)221 25 54 30

—Potsdam

Alexandra Fromm
Tuchmacherstraße 34, 14482 Potsdam
+49 (0)331 550 36 90

199

Black Market
Dortustraße 65, 14467 Potsdam
+49 (0)331 237 06 52

Easy Second Hand Shop
Lindenstraße 8, 14467 Potsdam
+49 (0)331 979 30 31

Second-Hand-Kaufhaus
Charlottenstraße 14, 14467 Potsdam
+49 (0)331 29 36 94

Whooppie
Hermann-Elflein-Straße 23, 14467 Potsdam
+49 (0)331 280 41 37

—Strausberg

Simone Pott
Bahnhofstraße 23, 15344 Strausberg
+49 (0)3341 47 65 24

Greece

—Athens

Vintage Clothing Sale
29a Agiou Markou Street, 105 60 Athens
+30 210 321 6337

Hungary

—Budapest

Bross Second Hand
Múzeum körút 23, 1056 Budapest
+36 (0)1 974 9355

Ciánkáli
Dohány utca 68, 1074 Budapest
+36 (0)1 341 0540

Ecseri Flea Market XIX
Nagykörösi út 156, 1194 Budapest

Egyedi Ruha Galeria
IX Baross utca 4, D-VIII, Budapest
+36 (0)1 118 2056

Garderobe
—Nagymezõ utca 36, 1065 Budapest
  +36 (0)1 269 2609
—Erzsébet körút 25–27, 1073 Budapest
  +36 (0)1 352 1973

Gizmo
—Múzeum körút 7, 1053 Budapest
  +36 (0)1 266 4660
—Oktogon, 1067 Budapest
  +36 (0)1 276 1483

Favourite piece? Schiaparelli torn dress. *This dress combined a fine-art collaboration Dalì-like surrealist print, which gave the illusion that the dress was torn in areas, with a sophisticated and glamorous evening dress. It optimised the use of a textile design that relates directly to the garment on which it is applied. It is a piece that has always stuck in my mind and inspired me.* **Favourite resource? Keni Valenti** *is a fantastic archive in New York. The space is rammed full with a mix of couture and also experimental pieces from the seventies and eighties. Every piece has a story as to how he acquired it. Also* **the V&A, London, has an incredible collection that spans from the nineteenth century to now.** *You can make an appointment to view certain pieces and the archivist will give you a history of the garment. This is where I saw the Schiaparelli dress.* **Future collectable? Any designer who uses an intricate or technical process,** *for example Hussein Chalayan.*

JONATHAN SAUNDERS
Designer

DIRECTORY

Józsefvárosi Piac III
Kóbányai út, Budapest
+36 (0)1 313 8890

Oké
—Múzeum körút 9, 1056 Budapest
+36 (0)1 266 1571
—Nagymezõ utca 47, 1065
Budapest
+36 (0)1 214 0173

Second Hand Szinte Új Ruhák
Párizsi utca 9, 1052 Budapest
+36 (0)1 318 7236

Tammy
Rumbach Sebestyén utca 3, 1075
Budapest
+36 (0)1 266 3122

Tweed
VI Dalszinhaz utca 10, Budapest
+36 (0)1 332 9294

Israel

—Tel Aviv

Miki & Tal's
13 King George Street, Tel Aviv
+972 (0)3 528 2848

Shuk Hapishp'shim (Flea Market)
Between Jerusalem Boulevard and
Yeffet Street, Tel Aviv

Yad Shnia
72 Ben Yehuda Street, Tel Aviv
+972 (0)3 527 6614

Italy

—Bologna

Piazzola (Mercato Montagnola)
Piazza VIII Agosto, Parco della
Montagnola, 40126 Bologna
+39 (0)51 35 94 23

Quo Vadis
Via di Corticella, 26, 40128 Bologna
+39 (0)51 35 94 23

—Florence

Echo
Via dell'Oriuolo, 37, Centro Storico,
Florence
+389 (0)55 238 11 49

—Genoa

Almanacco
Via Macelli di Soziglia, 41r, 16124
Genoa
+39 (0)10 26 56 05

Betty Page
Via Ravecca, 51r, 16123 Genoa
+39 (0)10 26 10 23

Fox Trot
Via Luccoli, 94r, 16123 Genoa
+39 (0)10 247 40 78

—Milan

A.N.G.E.L.O
Galleria Passerella, 2, 2012 Milan
+39 (0)2 760 06051
www.angelo.it
Angelo's vintage palace is one of the most prestigious vintage shops in Italy. Two floors are filled with haute couture and the most extensive collection of vintage Levi in Europe. There is also a 'bargain basement' of discounted pieces out in the courtyard. Also rents items from 50 euros and a large deposit.

Cavalli e Nastri
Via De Amicis, 9, 20123 Milan
+39 02 894 09452

Franco Jacassi
Via Sacchi, 3, 20121 Milan
+39 (0)2 864 62076

L'Armadio di Laura
Via Voghera, 25, 20144 Milan
+39 (0)2 836 0606

Mulino Docks Dora
Via Toffetti, 9, 20139 Milan
+39 (0)2 568 10393
www.docks-dora.com

—Palermo

Paternostro Pellice
Via Cataldo Parisio, 72a,
90145 Palermo
+39 (0)9 168 12108

—Parma

Vecchia America
Via Nazario Sauro, 7, 43100 Parma
+39 (0)5 212 35697
Sells Victorian tops, dresses that go right back to the Thirties and a great selection of cocktail hats.

—Rome

Bianco e Nero
Via Marrucini, 34, San Lorenzo,
Rome
+39 (0)6 44 50 286

Cecilia e Omero
Via del Governo Vecchio, 68,
00186 Rome
+39 (0)6 683 3506

DIRECTORY

Fabio Piccioni
Via del Boschetto, 148, 00184 Rome
+39 (0)6 474 1697

Fuoriserie
Via della Lungara, 42a, 00165 Rome
+39 (0)6 686 7732

Le Gallinelle
Via del Boschetto, 76, 00184 Rome
+39 (0)6 488 1017
www.legallinelle.it
This former butcher's shop now stocks a wealth of vintage clothing as well as some pieces that are new but made from vintage textiles. The clothes are interestingly displayed on the stores original meat hooks.

L'Oca Giuliva
Via Caroncini, 58, 00197 Rome
+39 (0)6 807 4829

Marcolino
Via Plauto, 16, 00193 Rome
+39 (0)6 686 5782

Rags Utd
Piazza Campo dei Fiori, 11/12, 00186 Rome
+39 (0)6 687 9344

Rigattieri per Hobby
Via Luciani, 54, 00197 Rome
+39 (0)6 321 6930

Tempi Moderni
Via del Governo Vecchio, 108, Rome
+39 (0)6 687 7007
One of the best vintage costume jewellery shops in Italy. The selection dates from 1880 right up to 1970 with great emphasis placed on Art Deco and Art Nouveau pieces. You can find nineteenth-century brooches as well as later designed jewellery from the likes of Lanvin, Balenciaga and Chanel.

—Verona

Abiti d'altri Tempi
Via Santa Maria in Chiavica, 3a, 37121 Verona
Based next to the historical centre of Verona, this vintage shop is small but surprisingly stocks a fantastic range of couture dresses from the Sixties and Seventies.

Japan
—Fukuoka

Hard to Find
Toho Building 105, 1-10-33 Daimyo, Chuo-ku, Fukuoka City, Fukuoka-ken, 810-0041
+81 (0)92 722 2747

Rug Machine
2-4-27-2F Imaizumi, Chuo-ku,
Fukuoka City, Fukuoka-ken, 810-0021
+81 (0)92 732 7530

—Kyoto

Konjyaku Nishimura
381 Moto-cho Yamato-oji higashi iru,
Furumonzen dori, Higashiyama-ku,
Kyoto, 605-0059
+81 (0)75 561 1312

Nakamura Chingire Ten
Sanjo minami-iru, Nawate dori
Higashiyama-ku, Kyoto, 605
+81 (0)75 561 4726

Bon Kyoto
Kitashirakawa Bettocho kado,
Sakyo-ku, Kyoto, 606-8277
+81 (0)75 711 7095

—Osaka

Kind
it Bldg 1-3F, 2-18-9 Nishi-
Shinsaibashi, Chuo-ku, Osaka, 542-
0086
+81 (0)6 6484

—Sapporo

Mamegura
Ikuei Bldg. 1F, Odori Nishi 14,
Sapporo, Hokkaido, 060-0042
+81 (0)11 272 6788

—Tokyo

A/T
20-20 Daikanyamacho, Shibuya-ku,
Ebisu/Daikanyama, Tokyo, 150-0034
+81 (0)3 5459 3810

Burdocks
1-17-5 Kamimeguro, Meguro, Tokyo
+81 (0)3 5768 7258
www.burdocks.com

Per Gramme Market &
Expedition Mode
Mori Building, 1-6-5 Kamimeguro,
Meguro-ku, Tokyo
+81 (0)3 3760 3777
With this vintage store, you get two for the price of one. On the ground floor, the Per Gramme market sells mainly Eighties' fashion such as cocktail dresses, batwing tops and sequinned tops. Everything is sold by the weight – 8 yen per gramme. Venture upstairs to Expedition Mode and you would be forgiven for thinking you were in a different shop. This floor is filled with the owner's European finds including dainty

Many of the designers that are going to be significant for the history of fashion are Japanese – *Rei Kawakubo of Comme des Garçons, her protégée Junya Watanabe and Yohji Yamamoto. These are at the forefront of avant-garde fashion. Other important names include Alexander McQueen, Rick Owen, Martin Margiela, Undercover, Boudicca and Dries van Noten. It is, however, more expensive to collect vintage pieces with big names so ultimately, go for pieces that are interesting but perhaps not so instantly recognisable.*

DR VALERIE STEELE
Chief Curator and Director, *The Museum – Fashion Institute of Technology, New York*

Victorian dresses and French designer labels that go back to the Fifties.

Par Avion
4-1-3 Minami Aoyama, Minato-ku, Tokyo
+81 (0)3 3470 6536

Chicago
—*Omotesando branch*
  6-31-21 Jingumae, Shibuya-ku
  +81 (0)3 3409 5017
—*Takeshita branch*
  1-6-7 Jingumae, Shibuya-ku
  +81 (0)3 3478 6285
—*Jingumae branch*
  1-6-1 Jingumae, Shibuya-ku
  +81 (0)3 3408 8482
—*Shimokitazawa branch*
  5-32-5 Daizawa, Setagaya-ku
  +81 (0)3 3419 2890
This Tokyo based store has four branches in the area. It stocks original Mackintosh jackets, Sixties' Pucci-esque dresses and a huge selection of vintage kimonos and obis.

G2
3-22-7 Jingumae, Shibuya-ku
+81 (0)3 5786 4188

Hiroki
2-96 Motomachi, Naka ku
Yokohama, Kanagawa-ken 231-0861
+81 (0)45 681 1335

No 44
Bellwood Harajuku 1C, 3-20-21 Jingumae, Shibuya-ku, Tokyo
+81 (0)3 3475 4044

Old Hat
6-34-14 Jingumae, Shibuya-ku, Tokyo 150-0001
+81 (0)3 3498 2956

Reminiscence
Kono Building 1F, 14-14 Udagawacho, Shibuya-ku, Tokyo 150-0042
+81 (0)3 5428 0120

Santa Monica
1-11-5 Jinnan, Shibuya-ku
+81 (0)3 3462 1984

Swipe
5-32-13 Daizawa, Setagaya-ku Shimokitazawa
+81 (0)3 3487 9027
This is a popular outlet for locals and visitors alike as there is a constant flow of new pieces for sale. The owner scours all over Europe and the USA as well as Japan for stock, which mainly derives from the Sixties.

We Go
—*Harajuku branch*
  6-5-3 Jingumae, Shibuya-ku
  +81 (0)3 3400 7625

—*Shimokitazawa branch*
2-26-7 Kitazawa, Setegaya-ku
+81 (0)3 5790 8451

Netherlands

—Amsterdam

La Rosa Curiosa
Spuistraat 181b, 1012 VN Amsterdam
+31 (0)20 638 61 18
www.larosacuriosa.com

Lady Day
Hartenstraat 9, 1016 BZ,
Amsterdam
+31 (0)20 623 58 20
Set up over 30 years ago in the trendy shopping district of De Negen Straatjes, Lady Day is the vintage establishment in Amsterdam. Stylists and bargain hunters alike frequent the store where they rummage through designs from the Fifties to the Seventies. Whether you are looking for retro trainers or a dress for a black-tie function, Lady Day has something to fit every occasion.

Laura Dols
Wolvenstraat 6&7, 1016 EM,
Amsterdam
+31 (0)20 624 90 66
www.lauradols.nl

This popular vintage shop specialises in vintage clothing from the Twenties to the Seventies. One section of the store focuses on eveningwear for men and women whilst another section caters for customers more interested in daywear. Also stocks a good selection of children's clothes.

Ree-member
Reestraat 26, 1016 DN, Amsterdam
+31 (0)20 622 13 29
Ree-member stocks a wide range of mainly Seventies' vintage clothing and is generally seen as the best place to buy vintage shoes in Amsterdam. A little pricey but less than perfect pieces can be bought much cheaper at the Noordermarkt (flea market). Their stock here is sold by the kilo.

Wini
Haarlemmerstraat 29, 1013 EJ,
Amsterdam
+31 (0)20 427 9393

Zipper
Huidenstraat 7, 1016 ER,
Amsterdam
+31 (0)20 623 73 02

New Zealand

—Auckland

Back Again Boutique
3085 Great North Road, New Lynn,
Auckland
+64 (0)9 827 1221

Bizarre
363 Dominion Road, Mount Eden,
Auckland
+64 (0)9 630 0092

Fuzzy Vibes Junction
151 Karangahape Road, Newton,
Auckland
+64 (0)9 309 1451

Peachy Keen
374 Karangahape Road, Auckland
+64 (0)9 377 2733

Smith & Roelants
Shop 9, St. Kevin's Arcade,
183 Karangahape Road, Auckland
+64 (0)9 309 3375

This is Not a Love Shop
217b Dominion Road, Mount Eden,
Auckland
+64 (0)9 630 5563

—Christchurch

Forget Me Nots Antiques
167 High Street, Christchurch
+64 (0)3 365 3375

Gertie's Vintage Clothing
162 High Street, Christchurch
+64 (0)3 365 1221

Hunters & Collectors
177 Manchester Street, Christchurch
+64 (0)3 365 3751

Preloved Clothing
1 Milton Street, Christchurch
+64 (0)3 332 0289

Tete a Tete
88 Hereford Street, Christchurch
+64 (0)3 366 5442

—Wellington

Frutti
166 Cuba Street, Wellington
+64 (0)4 384 6965

Past & Present
101 Cuba Street, Wellington
+64 (0)4 384 1405

DIRECTORY

Norway

—Oslo

American Classics
Grensen 9, 0159 Oslo
+47 22 41 39 88

Underground
Storgaten 1, 0184 Oslo
+47 22 42 09 66

Poland

—Krakow

Hala Targowa
Ulica Grzegórzecka, Krakow
31-532
+48 12 421 77 06
www.grzegorzecka.glt.pl

—Warsaw

3 x Super
Ulica Nowowiejska, 4, Warsaw 00-649
+48 22 629 19 61

Retro 70
Ulica Chmielna, Warsaw
+48 22 828 03 39

Retro-Future
Aleja Solidarno´sci, 82, Warsaw
00-145
+48 22 828 94 98

Russia

—Moscow

Brocade
Inside Gostiny Dvor, 3 Varavka Ul.,
Moscow
+7 (095) 298 10 21
Owned by one of Russia's premier fashion collectors, Brocade is a top-end vintage store offering pieces from the likes of Paul Poiret and Christian Dior as well as Thirties' dresses and silk Oriental robes.

Frik Frak
25/1 Shabolovskaya Ul., 117049
Moscow
+7 (095) 164 91 00

Garderob Weekend
24/1 Bolshaya Nikitskaya Ul.,
Moscow
+7 (095) 202 73 83

Pavel Elion
+7 (095) 942 96 26
www.pelion.ru

Soho
23 Kutuzovsky Pr., Moscow
+7 (095) 249 58 26

Zima
4 Vorotnikovsky Per., Moscow
+7 (095) 209 37 25
www.izima.ru

Spain

—Barcelona

Argot
Carrer de l'Hospital, 107, Barcelona

Erreté
Riera Baixa, 10, 08001 Barcelona
+34 93 329 62 00

Holala
Riera Baixa, 11, 08001 Barcelona

Lailo
Carrer de la Riera Baixa, 20, 08001
Barcelona
+34 93 441 37 49

Mánodos
Carme, 39, Barcelona

Mies & Felj
Carrer de la Riera Baixa, 4, 08001
Barcelona
+34 93 442 07 55

Recicla Recicla
Carrer de la Riera Baixa, 13, 08001
Barcelona
+34 93 443 18 15

—Bilbao

Amsterdam Plein
Plaza Nueva, 11, 48005 Bilbao
+34 94 415 88 72

—Madrid

Boo Yaa
Hortaleza, 3, 28004 Madrid
+34 91 523 45 35

Cristina Guisado
Doctor Fourquet, 10, 28012 Madrid
+34 91 528 87 88

El Rastro
Calle Ribera de Curtidores, Madrid

La Latina & Lavapies
Mira el Río Baja, 13, 28005 Madrid
+34 91 467 24 52

DIRECTORY

Underground Moda
Mira el Río Baja, 14, 28005 Madrid
+34 91 364 15 46

—San Sebastian

Bric a Brac
San Jerónimo, 12, San Sebastián-
Donostia, Guipúzcoa 20003, San
Sebastian
+34 94 342 53 60

DAM
Narrica, 23, San Sebastián-
Donostia, Guipúzcoa 20003, San
Sebastian
+34 94 342 45 67

Marigorri
Aldamar, 10, San Sebastián-
Donostia, Guipúzcoa 20003,
San Sebastian
+34 94 342 57 81

—Valencia

Ropero
San Vicente, 25, 46002 Valencia
+34 655 850 282

—Zaragoza

A Todo Trapo
Méndez Núñez, 9, 50003 Zaragoza
+34 976 29 77 47

Rastro de la Plaza de Toros
Glorieta de José Aznarez, 50004
Zaragoza

—Balearics/Ibiza

Ganesha
Calle Montgri, 14, Ibiza
+34 971 193 605

Holala
Plaza del Mercado Viejo, 12, 07800
Ibiza
+34 971 316 537
www.holala-ibiza.com

Sweden

—Stockholm

118 Second Läder
Odengatan 86, 113 22 Stockholm
+46 (0)8 34 20 59

59 Vintage Store
Hantverkargatan 59, 112 31
Stockholm
+46 (0)8 652 37 27

Anneritas Second Hand
Essinge Brogatan 5, 112 61
Stockholm
+46 (0)8 656 33 73

A vintage shopper is like a bounty hunter, *only this crusade ends on a quest for style. The Holy Grail: the unworn Ossie or graduate piece from Galliano. Like a magpie, these are rare sightings, but when it happens, it makes the rush twice that of paragliding off a cliff.*

CAMILLA MORTON
Author of best-selling book
How to Walk in High Heels

DIRECTORY

Beyond Retro
Asögatan 114, 116 24 Stockholm
+46 (0)8 641 36 42

Birgitta's Second Hand
Sibyllegatan 63, 114 43 Stockholm
+46 (0)8 665 60 06

Camilla's Kläder Second Hand & Nytt
Fleminggatan 28,
+46 (0)8 652 35 40

Chanesse
Grev Turegatan 1, 114 46 Stockholm
+46 (0)8 611 31 72

Damaged Goods
Birkagatan 14, 113 39 Stockholm
+46 (0)7 06631498
www.damagedgoods.se

Ditt & Datt Second Hand
Ålstensgatan 15, 167 17 Bromma
+46 (0)8 634 02 20

Emmaus
Götgatan 14, 118 46 Stockholm
+46 (0)8 644 85 86
www.emmaus.aos.se

Epok
Odengatan 83, 113 22 Stockholm
+46 (0)8 34 13 40

Flea Market
Bottenvåningen Vårberg Centrum,
127 23 Stockholm
+46 (0)8 710 00 60
www.loppmarknaden.se

Habiiba
Södermannagatan 18, 116 23
Stockholm
+46 (0)8 644 80 06

Helene Thörnsten
Torsgatan 57, 113 37 Stockholm
+46 (0)8 31 38 25

Jennys Stil
Södermannagatan 18, 116 23
Stockholm
+46 (0)8 644 80 06

Judits Second Hand
Hornsgatan 75, 118 49 Stockholm
+46 (0)8 84 45 10
www.judits.se

Kameleonten
Wittstocksgatan 6, 115 24 Stockholm
+46 (0)8 663 61 90

La Principessa
Rosenlundsgatan 1, 118 53 Stockholm
+46 (0)8 658 44 60
www.la-principessa.net

Lisa Larsson Second Hand
Bondegatan 48, 116 33 Stockholm
+46 (0)8 643 61 53

Myrorna
Kolargatan 2, 100 54 Stockholm
+46 (0)8 545 844 66
www.myrorna.se

Old Touch
Upplandsgatan 43, 113 28 Stockholm
+46 (0)8 349 005

Påkläderiet
Södermannagatan 21, 116 40
Stockholm
+46 (0)8 462 91 90

Repris,
Bondegatan 48, 116 33 Stockholm
+46 (0)8 640 25 48
www.repris-stockholm.se

Röda Korset
Östgötagatan 65, 116 64 Stockholm
+46 (0)8 702 08 40

Ruby's Vintage Clothing
Wollmar Yxkullsgatan 10, 118 48
Stockholm
+46 (0)8 643 20 51

Saker Och Ting
Sturegatan 28, 114 36 Stockholm
+46 (0)8 667 37 63

Say Hello to my Little Friend
Torsgatan 40, 113 62 Stockholm
+46 (0)70 832 98 02

Second Hand Rose
Hornsgatan 29a, 118 49 Stockholm
+46 (0)8 643 19 19

Skärholmens Loppmarknad
(Flea Market)
Parkeringshuset,
Skärholmens, Stockholm

Sko Dig (shoes)
Hagagatan 4, 113 48 Stockholm
+46 (0)8 33 74 74

Söder Teknik Second Hand
Folkungagatan 87, 116 30
Stockholm
+46 (0)8 643 34 51

Stadsmission Second Hand
Hantverkargatan 78, 112 38
Stockholm
+46 (0)8 65 27 475
www.stadsmissionen.se

SVART
Bondegatan 1f, 116 23 Stockholm
+46 (0)8 644 86 35
www.svartsthlm.se

Tant Gerdelins Garderob
Karlavägen 72, 114 59 Stockholm
+46 (0)8 662 17 50

Två Tre Gånger
Hornsgatan 39, 118 20 Stockholm

Vilse I Garderoben
Hantverkargatan 59, 112 31
Stockholm
+46 (0)8 652 37 27

Switzerland

—Basel

Kangaroo
Andreasplatz 7, Imbergässlein Basel,
Basel-Stadt 4051
+41 61 261 59 09

Taiwan

—Taipei

E-Heaven
53 Lane 187, Dun Hua South Road,
Section 1, Ta An District, Taipei
TW, 106
+886 (0)2 2771 4871

Cola Forest
2 Lane 114, Zhong Hua Road,
Section 1, Wan Hua District, Taipei
TW, 108
+886 (0)2 2370 2013

Hippie Village
2F, 2 Lane 82, Wu Chang Street,
Section 2, Wan Hua District, Taipei
TW, 108
+886 (0)2 2389 2702

Polar Star
2F, 7 Lane 50, Xi Ning South Road
Wan Hua District, Taipei TW, 108
+886 (0)2 2388 3861

Take Two
13 Lane 96, Kun Ming Street, Wan
Hua District, Taipei TW, 108
+886 (0)2 2388 6182

Turkey

—Istanbul

Avant-Garde East & Retro
Fourth Floor, Istiklal Caddesi, Suriye
Pasaji, 230/12, Beyoglu, Istanbul
+90 (0)212 245 15 07

Porto Bella
Cihangir Caddesi 29, Beyoglu, Istanbul
+90 (0)212 292 71 23/24

Pulp
Istiklal Caddesi, Atlas Pasaji,
209/42, Beyoglu, Istanbul
+90 (0)212 244 34 20

Roxy
Istiklal Caddesi, Aznavur Pasaji,
212/11, Beyoglu, Istanbul
+90 (0)212 244 33 63

Stage
Istiklal Caddesi, Suriye Pasaji,
348/4, Istanbul
+90 (0)212 244 94 76

Ve Saire
Doktor Faruk Ayanoglu Caddesi,
Karika Sokak, 31, Kalamis, Istanbul
+90 (0)216 338 35 40

United Kingdom

England

—Bath

Collectable Costume
Fountain Antiques Centre,
3 Fountain Buildings, Lansdowne
Road, Bath BA1 5DU
+44 (0)1225 428 731

Fountain Antiques Centre
3 Fountain Building, Lansdown Road,
Bath BA1 5DU
+44 (0)1225 428 731

Jack & Danny's
Walcot Street, Bath BA1 5BN
+44 (0)1225 312 345

The Shaw Trust
11 George Street, Bath BA1 2EH
+44 (0)1225 460 225
www.shaw-trust.org.uk

Vintage to Vogue
28 Milsom Street, Bath BA1 1DG
+44 (0)1225 337 323

—Birmingham

Covet
The Custard Factory, Gibb Square,
Birmingham B9 4AA
+44 (0)121 224 8281

Gladrags
3 Ethel Street, Birmingham B2 4BG
+44 (0)121 633 3239

Juice
The Arcadian Centre, Hurst Street,
Birmingham B5 4TD
+44 (0)121 622 4565

DIRECTORY

Moseley Vintage Clothes Fair
Moseley Community Centre,
The Post Office Building,
149–153 Alcester Road, Moseley,
Birmingham B13 8JP

Retro Bizarre
25 St Mary's Row, Moseley,
Birmingham B13 8HW
+44 (0)121 442 6389

Urban Village
86 Hurst Street, Birmingham B5 4TD
+44 (0)121 622 5351

—Blackburn

Decades
20 Lord Street West, Blackburn
BB2 1JX
+44 (0)1254 693 320
www.decadesemporium.co.uk

—Brighton

30a Upper St James's Street
30a Upper St James's Street,
Brighton BN2 1JN
+44 (0)1273 681 384

Dolly
46 Sydney Street, North Laine,
Brighton BN1 4EP
+44 (0)1273 693 506

Harlequin Vintage
31 Sydney Street, North Laine,
Brighton BN1 4EP
+44 (0)1273 675 222
www.harlequin-vintage.co.uk

Rokit
23 Kensington Gardens, North Laine,
Brighton BN1 4AL
+44 (0)1273 672 053
www.rokit.co.uk

StarFish
25 Gardner Street, North Laine,
Brighton BN1 1UP
+44 (0)1273 690 035

Yellow Submarine
12 Kensington Gardens, Brighton
BN1 4AL
+44 (0)1273 626 435

—Bristol

Clifton Hill Antique Costume &
Textiles
5 Lower Clifton Hill, Clifton, Bristol
BS8 1BT
+44 (0)117 929 0644

Katze
55 Gloucester Road, Bishopston,
Bristol BS7 8AD
+44 (0)117 942 5625

Cornucopia

Where? 12 Upper Tachbrook Street, Pimlico, London SW1V 1SH   +44 (0)20 7828 5752

Why go there? Very close to Victoria station, this is a centrally located store with the charms of an old village shop.

What's it like? The window display is a real draw into the store. Elegant Twenties' sequin capes are draped over sophisticated mannequins topped with Fifties' hats. When you step inside, the celestial feeling that drew you in is replaced with one that makes you want to take a deep breath and roll up your sleeves. There is an impressive mixed bag of clothing and accessories on display everywhere. Definitely not for anyone suffering from claustrophobia.

Best for? Cocktail dresses/eveningwear, bags – from beaded to croc skin – amazing brooches, fur capes, lingerie and coats… The vastness of the collection means this shop excels in almost every area of clothing.

Clientele? From the 55-year old lady who lives around the corner to the well-connected man who owns a respected vintage shop in London. Stylists love Cornucopia not just for the amazing finds but because there is no restriction on the amount of pieces you can loan for a shoot.

Hot tip? Everything is sorted according to style, which makes it easier to concentrate on the type of clothing you're after. Haggling, it seems, is not a cardinal sin so take full advantage, especially when purchasing more than two items and anything not in mint condition. Here the emphasis is on pieces that typify an era as opposed to actual labels, but keep your eyes peeled as you might stumble across a fashion rarity.

Prices? Some of the best prices in London, such as a Fifties' gold damask dress (which could have inspired a past Prada collection) priced at £35, a Sixties' turquoise summer coat at £20 and a Twenties' beaded dress at £200. Jewellery and cocktail hats start from £10; dresses are anything from £15 and pretty silk camisole tops are £12.

219

DIRECTORY

RePsycho
85 Gloucester Road, Bishopston,
Bristol BS7 8AS
+44 (0)117 983 0007

Uncle Sam's
54a Park Street, Bristol BS1 5JN
+44 (0)117 929 8404

—Burton-on-Trent

Back in Fashion
38 High Street, Tutbury, Burton-on-
Trent DE13 9LS
+44 (0)1283 814 964

—Dorking

Shrewd
82–84 High Street, Dorking RH4 1AY
+44 (0)1306 889 099
www.shrewd.biz

—Exeter

The Real McCoy
21 The Fore Street Centre, Fore
Street, Exeter EX4 3AN
+44 (0)1392 410 481
www.therealmccoy.co.uk

—Hythe

Bohemia
104 High Street, Hythe, Kent
+44 (0)1303 267 020
www.vintagebohemia.co.uk

—Leeds

Blue Rinse
9 & 11 Call Lane, Leeds LS1 7DH
+44 (0)1132 451 735

—Lincoln

Patricia Rowberry
Antiques & Collectables Centre,
64–65 Steephill, Lincoln LN1 1YN
+44 (0)1522 545 916

—Liverpool

Treasures in Textiles
53 Russian Drive, Tuebrook,
Liverpool L13 7BS
+44 (0)151 281 602

Vintage Clothing Company
Quiggins Centre, 12–16 School
Lane, Liverpool L1 3BT
+44 (0)151 709 2462

—Central London

Blackout II
*51 Endell Street, Covent Garden,
London WC2H 9HJ*
+44 (0)20 7240 5006
www.blackout2.com
Although close to Covent Garden, Blackout II's Endell Street location is a welcome respite the high-street. Compact yet comprehensive, this store is spread over two floors. The rooms are small and you have to crouch low to the lower floor. This is easily forgiven when you see the selection on offer. Pieces span from the Twenties to the Eighties and shoes, in particular, are a good buy, starting from about £35.

Grays Antique Markets
*1–7 Davies Mews & 58 Davies
Street, London W1K 5AB*
+44 (0)20 7629 7034
www.graysantiques.com

Harvey Nichols
*109–125 Knightsbridge, London
SW1X 7J*
+44 (0)20 7235 5000
www.harveynichols.com

Jennifer Smit Vintage
+44 (0)7790 772 461
www.jennifersmit.com

If there is anyone who has recently become the name to have in your address book, it is this woman. Jennifer Smit has been in vintage for less than three years, yet she's giving other dealers a run for their money. Smit travels a number of times a year – mainly across America – to collect exquisite pieces that she sells to clients through her chic Bayswater apartment. From time to time she has rare pieces from the likes of Dior and Pucci, yet she is more interested in seeking out pieces that are a part of fashion history than designer labels. She follows the collections every season and tailors her vintage buys to compliment whatever is going on in fashion at that point in time. Clients can request particular items they are interested in, which Smit makes the effort to locate. Though Smit's clients include Kate Moss and others who have an endless pit of money, her prices are still very reasonable.

Linda Bee
*Stand L18, Grays Antiques Market,
1–7 Davies Mews, London W1K 5AB*
+44 (0)20 7629 5921

Marshmallow Mountain
*Ground Floor, Kingly Court,
49 Carnaby Street, London W1*
+44 (0)20 7434 9498
www.marshmellowmountain.com

Frock Me!

Where? Chelsea Town Hall, King's Road, Chelsea, London SW3 5EZ, +44 (0)20 7254 4054
www.frockmevintagefashion.com

Why go there? Unlike other key fairs in the city, this one is based in Central London so is easy to get to. This recently revived fair showcases an array of clothing from the Edwardian period up to the Seventies.

What's it like? Once you've walked up the entrance stairs, gone through the formal, old-fashioned hallway and past the serious-looking library, this is where any type of conservatism ends. As soon as you hit the actual entrance to the fair, you are faced with the dilemma of where to go first. There is a plethora of beautiful pieces to look at in this buzzing setting so unless you spend a few hours there, you will inevitably miss something. All the stalls are very much individual. Many hold pieces from the Sixties and Seventies and a number specialise in specific designers or eras. One stallholder in particular carries mainly antique textiles and clothing from the Belle Époque and has fabulous mannequins displaying her wares. On the other hand, C20 Vintage Fashion has a huge collection of Ossie Clark. Stalls are not placed together bumper-to-bumper making it easy to flit from one to another. From frockcoats to fur coats, handbags to Halston, there is something to meet every need.

Best for? Victoriana pieces, fur capes, Seventies' fashion, including collectable Ossie Clark, costume jewellery and fabulous hats.

Clientele? Chelsea girls who are keen to individualise their look, vintage-hungry fashionistas, designers and the like.

Hot tip? Either get there early in order to pick up the best pieces or get there towards the end of the day in order to up the bargains. For obvious reasons, dealers don't want to leave the fair with as many pieces as they came with; towards the end of the day, they are most likely to accept an offer of a lower price.

Pop Boutique

6 Monmouth Street, Covent Garden,
London WC2H 9HB
+44 (0)20 7497 5262
www.pop-boutique.com

A favourite with students and those interested in vintage day wear, Pop Boutique stocks 'Retro' as opposed to period clothing. Part of the Vintage Clothing Company, Pop carries vintage Levi's and other denim labels, corduroy trousers, psychedelic print Seventies' dresses, a vast selection of Eighties' belts and other kitsch pieces. Lively and kooky, you're unlikely to discover a serious collector's item here but it is nevertheless a fun place to shop.

Sam Greenberg

Unit 1.7, Kingly Court, 49 Carnaby
Street, London W1B 5PW
+44 (0)20 7287 8474
www.samgreenbergrnwl.co.uk

TopShop Vintage

214 Oxford Street, London W1W 8LG
+44 (0)20 7636 7700
www.topshop.co.uk

As the vintage market has expanded, this section has cleverly expanded with the trend. Within the basement of the 'world's largest fashion store', the bulk of vintage is made up almost entirely of pieces from the Fifties onwards. If you are looking for Bohemian clothing for daywear, Petticoat is your best bet to pick up beautiful Seventies' cheesecloth dresses that start from £45 and leather bags from £25. Another label, Dolly Rockers specialises in velvet and leather jackets from £30 while Vintage Princess offers a range of cocktail dresses as well as the odd piece from the Twenties and Thirties.

—East London

Absolute Vintage

15 Hanbury Street, London E1 6Q
+44 (0)20 7247 3883
www.absolutevintage.co.uk

Beyond Retro

110–112 Cheshire Street,
Shoreditch, London E2 6EJ
+44 (0)20 7613 3636
www.beyondretro.com

Rokit

—101 Brick Lane, London E1 6SE
  +44 (0)20 7375 3864
—225 Camden High Street,
  Camden, London NW1 7BU
  +44 (0)20 7267 3046
—42 Shelton Street, Covent Garden,
  London WC2 9HZ
  +44 (0) 7836 6547
www.rokit.co.uk

This shop, located on East London's Brick Lane, typifies what is known as

DIRECTORY

Hoxton Chic – über cool, very retro but with a touch of grunge. Specialising in clothes mainly from the Seventies and Eighties, it is the perfect place to find tooled bags, Eighties' shoes and belts and fabulous cowboy boots, which start from £35. Branches also in Camden, North London, Covent Garden, Central London and Brighton, East Sussex.

—North London

162
162 Holloway Road, London N7 8DQ

Annie's
*12 Camden Passage, Islington,
London N1 8ED
+44 (0)20 7359 0796*

Biba Lives at Alfies Antique Market
*13–25 Church Street, Marylebone,
London NW8 8DT
+44 (0)20 7258 7999
www.bibalives.com*

Cloud Cuckoo Land
*6 Charlton Place, Camden Passage,
Islington, London N1 8ED
+44 (0)20 7354 3141*

Dolly Rockers
*16–18 Stables Market, Chalk Farm
Road, Camden, London NW1 2PB
+44 (0)20 7482 0193*

Gallery of Antique Costume & Textiles
*2 Church Street, Marylebone,
London NW8 8ED
+44 (0)20 7723 9981*

The Girl Can't Help It at Alfies
Antique Market
*Stand G082, 13–25 Church Street,
Marylebone, London NW8 8DT
+44 (0)20 7724 8984
www.sparklemoore.com*

The Glamour Palace
*211 Woodhouse Road, North
Finchley, London N12 9AY
+44 (0)20 8368 2117*

Henry & Daughter
*17–18 Camden Lock Place, Camden,
London NW1 8AF
+44 (0)20 7284 3302*

Modern Age Vintage Clothing
*65 Chalk Farm Road, Chalk Farm,
London NW1 8AN
+44 (0)20 7482 3787*

Past Caring
*76 Essex Road, Islington, London
N1 8LT*

Stitch Up
*45 Parkway, Camden Town, London
NW1 7PN
+44 (0)20 7482 4404*

Steinberg & Tolkien

Where? 193 Kings Road, Chelsea, London SW3
+44 (0)20 7376 3660

Why go there? As the biggest vintage emporium in the UK, with one of the world's largest collections of couture, Steinberg & Tolkien's place in the vintage hall of fame is thoroughly deserved. Run by brother and sister Mark Steinberg and Tracey Tolkien, this shop stocks a vast range of influential designers and is the last word on costume jewellery. Helpful staff, who possess an enviable knowledge of vintage fashion.

What's it like? Set over two floors, the store is an exhibition in itself. To the untrained eye it is a mass of clutter, but for those who love to rummage – a prerequisite for any vintage lover – this store is heaven.

Best for? Beautiful and rare items such as Pucci and Dior pieces on their original hangers, a signed Warhol dress, Poiret couture, Trifari and Haskell jewellery. S&T is known for an extensive collection of eveningwear.

Clientele? Frequented by vintage aficionados, anyone who is anyone (Kate Moss, Nicole Kidman, Chloe Sevigny) and designers such as John Galliano and Tom Ford to acquire inspiration for their collections.

Hot tip? Visit on weekdays – first thing in the morning – as weekends tend to be busy and this, teemed with the gargantuan amount of clothes and jewellery, doesn't allow for easy browsing.

Prices? Original – and sometimes signed – designs from Givenchy, Balenciaga and Schiaparelli are no strangers to this store, therefore prices are unsurprisingly high. An original, immaculate Fortuny gown can fetch thousands of pounds while the cheapest Pucci dresses start from £400. It is still possible to find more affordable pieces – dresses from lesser-known designers are priced from £75, while Trifari and Haskell pieces start from £35. Every so often a sale takes place, which sees accessories such as bags and belts slashed to as little as £10.

Circa Vintage

Where? 8 Fulham High Street, Fulham, London SW6 3LQ, +44 (0)20 7736 5038
www.circavintage.com

Why go there? Set up by Maryann Sundholm and her daughter Astrid, this six-year-old shop is one of the biggest insider secrets in vintage fashion. Circa Vintage has a very personal and genuine touch. Maryann's unequivocal wisdom in vintage fashion guarantees you leave with a fabulous piece of clothing as well as a PhD in fashion history.

What's it like? The Japanese kimono-inspired design in the front of the shop is the first piece to stimulate your senses, but on entering the split-level boutique you are wowed even further. Unlike most vintage shops, it is ordered. A total clutter-free zone without aspiring to minimalism. The red carpet is so vivid it could be mistaken for a sea of velvet. This in addition to the fantastic old-school music, the comfy red sofa and the offers of tea and drinks makes Circa Vintage a celestial shop. The biggest fashion stylists in the world love this shop. Charlotte Stockdale, Katie Grand, Karl Plewka… Kate Moss has been known to sit on the carpet crossed legged with a bottle of wine in hand, such is the relaxed atmosphere. Call ahead to make an appointment.

Best for? Thea Porter, Ossie Clark and Biba.

Hot tip? If you are looking for something in particular, just ask. Maryann and Astrid have an incredible vintage collection that is kept off the sales floor. Shown to avid collectors they include very rare Ossie Clark and Celia Birtwell pieces – one from his graduate collection, apparently the only piece in existence. Also amongst her treasure trove is some very rare original fabric from a 1911 Paul Poiret gown and some quintessential Jean Varon pleated dresses.

Prices? Anything from £65 for a Forties' dress to £2,500 for a Thea Porter kaftan and ceremonial vintage kimonos.

—South London

Butler & Wilson
—189 Fulham Road, South
Kensington, London SW3 6JN
+44 (0)20 7352 3045
—20 South Molton Street, London
W1K 5QY
+44 (0)20 7409 0872
www.butlerandwilson.co.uk
Although this shop has two branches
in London, the Fulham Road shop is
much bigger and therefore has a much
more comprehensive range of clothing,
accessories and jewellery. B&W is
fantastic for exquisite jewellery from
the likes of Stanley Hagler and Miriam
Haskell, vintage kimonos, beaded
bags and Mexican hand-painted skirts.

Cenci
4 Nettlefold Place, West Norwood,
London SE27 0JW
+44 (0)20 8766 8564
www.cenci.co.uk

Emma Barker at Antiquarius
Unit V10, 131–141 Kings Road,
Chelsea, London SW3 4PW
+44 (0)7900 246 787
www.antiquarius.co.uk

The Emporium
330–332 Creek Road, Greenwich
Village, London SE10 8NW
+44 (0)20 8305 1670
www.emporiumoriginals.com

Nostalgia
57 Queenstown Rd, Battersea,
London SW8 3RG
+44 (0)20 7738 8777

The Observatory
20 Greenwich Church Street,
Greenwich Village, London SE10 9BJ
+44 (0)20 8305 1998 .

Radio Days
87 Lower Marsh, Waterloo, London
SE1 7AB
+44 (0)20 7928 0800
www.radiodaysvintage.co.uk

Traid
—2 Acre Lane, Brixton,
London SW2 5SG
+44 (0)20 7326 4330
—61 Westbourne Grove, Notting
Hill, London W2 4UA
+44 (0)20 7221 2421
www.traid.org.uk
The area of Brixton in South London is
renown for many things, vintage is not
one of them. This is why this upscale
charity shop – for want of a better word
– is such a welcome surprise. Situated

DIRECTORY

Whenever you buy delicate antique or vintage pieces, the first thing you should do is wash them or get them dry-cleaned to make sure there are no moths in them. **Moths really are a clothes killer**. *Also, never hang anything sequined or beaded – it's the worst thing you can do to them. Instead, lay it out in tissue paper and roll it and put it in a drawer or a box. This is the best way to maintain the original shape of the garment.*

VIRGINIA BATES
Owner of *Virginia's* in Holland Park, London

Virginia

Where? 98 Portland Road, Holland Park,
London W11 4LQ   +44 (0)20 7727 9908

Why go there? Run by ex-actress Virginia Bates, this boutique's reputation precedes it. Having acquired a reputation as one of the most expensive vintage shops in London, it's well worth the visit to see what the fuss is about.

What's it like? Spread over two floors, the exquisite store totally encapsulates a bygone era so rarely seen nowadays. Stocking restored period clothing and accessories from pre-Victorian times to the Forties, the walls are adorned with Victoriana petticoats, corsets, delicate chiffon lingerie from the Thirties and dresses worthy of any red carpet affair. Put it this way, a visit to Virginia's can be likened to stepping into a gasp-inducing fairy tale.

Best for? Victorian pieces, glamorous eveningwear, vintage wedding dresses, lingerie, iconic pieces from Yves Saint Laurent and Christian Dior.

Clientele? This is a key destination for serious collectors, fashion students and anyone who ha a large disposable income or simply love beautiful pieces at any cost. Many high-profile designers pay Virginia's very regular visits.

Hot tip? Opening times are slightly erratic so call before you visit. Also be very careful when handling the clothes in the store, as some of the pieces are particularly fragile.

Prices? This really is the top end of the vintage market. Don't expect to pay less than £100 for accessories – and that's just the beginning. Dresses go up to thousands of pounds. Virginia is known for her amazing restoration skills on pieces that were in less than perfect condition. The time and effort put into restoring the clothes are therefore reflected in her prices.

on the corner of Brixton Road and Acre Lane, this second-hand shop sets apart the vintage clothing at the far end of the store. A green Fifties' Pucci-esque dress was on sale for £14, a Thirties' evening clutch bag, £7 and a Sixties' printed summer coat £19. Although, there is another branch in West London at Notting Hill, be aware that the prices and stock do differ. And yes, the West London branch is pretty expensive for a charity shop, however buying a beautiful vintage piece and helping a worthy cause is not such a bad thing.

Old Hat

66 Fulham High Street, Fulham, London SW6 3LQ
+44 (0)20 7610 6558
Open for over 5 years, Old Hat started out catering for men with a penchant for quintessential British labels. Nowadays, in addition to those classics, you can get your hands on beautiful pieces from the wardrobes of some of the world's richest women. You could be forgiven for thinking that this store is an archaic gentlemen's outfitters: the windows are filled with bowler hats and traditional menswear that wouldn't look out of place on Saville Row in 1935. Don't be fooled. When you go up the old wooden staircase towards the back of the store, there is a wonderful array of womenswear from Chanel, Ted Lapidus, Christian Dior and a keen selection of Pierre Weyeneth dresses. Frequented by a kooky mix of customers, Old Hat has a special place in the hearts of visiting Japanese, which isn't that strange when you find out that the huge success of the Tokyo branch has elevated owner David Saxby to superstar level. Other customers include a number of women with blue blood running through their veins, Chanel collectors and men who want the perfect nostalgic outfit for the yearly Goodwood Racing Revival where everyone dresses in Forties' clothing. Be prepared to shop in a charming but slightly chaotic environment. It does look like they have always meant to tidy up but never quite got round to it and browsing can be pretty hazardous. However, keep in mind that there are diamonds to be found in the rough. Where else can you buy an amazing Chanel dress in pristine condition at £300? Forties' cotton dresses cost from £45 while Jermyn Street men shirts cost from £15. At the higher end of the scale, vintage kimono dresses cost from £250. A much coveted Louis Vuitton suitcase is £350, however, a dead stock version of this case – one that is vintage but unused – can cost up to £650.

What the Butler Wore
131 Lower Marsh Terrace, Waterloo,
London SE1 7AE
+44 (0)20 7261 1353
www.whatthebutlerwore.co.uk

—West London

The Antique Clothing Shop
282 Portobello Road, Notting
Hill, London W10 5TE
+44 (0)20 8964 4830 / 8993 4162
Absolutely fantastic for Victorian period clothing. This shop holds some very beautiful and unique pieces that are in a class of their own. The shop opened in 1993 and over the years its owner, Sandy Stagg, has taken on an almost legendary status. In spite of the grandeur that's been bestowed unto her, she still works in the store and is extremely helpful to customers. Take a deep breath. To say it is cluttered is an understatement. Clothes, shoes and bags are hanging from pillar to post. Even getting into the shop is somewhat dramatic as the front of the store is also festooned with a complete wardrobe of clothing. Clothes are split by era, however in the midst of such mass, if anything is regimented, it is rarely clear-cut. This is what is known as organised chaos. Best for fragile Victorian cotton tops and Edwardian lace silk. Accessories such as beaded purses are also a good buy here. Anyone who loves Victorian clothes. This place is famed for its Japanese customers and collection of vintage wedding dresses. The focus here is less on labels and concentrates more on the fashions of a particular era so don't spend hours – which is what you possibly need in this shop – looking for that elusive Jean Dessès piece. The prices here are very affordable, as they do not recondition. A Victorian lace-trimmed top starts from £80 while a Twenties' silk beaded flapper dress in immaculate condition will cost you £750.

Appleby
95 Westbourne Park Villas, Notting
Hill, London W2 5ED
+44 (0)20 7229 7772
www.applebyvintage.com

Dolly Diamond
51 Pembridge Road, Notting Hill,
London W11 3HG
+44 (0)20 7792 2479
www.dollydiamond.com

One of a Kind
253/259 Portobello Road, Notting
Hill, London W11 1LP
+44 (0)20 7792 5284

Rellik
8 Golborne Road, Notting Hill,
London W10 5NW
+44 (0)20 8962 0089

Sheila Cook Textiles
105–107 Portobello Road Notting
Hill, London W11 2 QB
+44 (0)20 7792 8001
www.sheilacook.co.uk

Still
61d Lancaster Road, Notting Hill,
London W11 1QG
+44 (0)20 7243 2932
A mere baby in comparison to its
Portobello counterparts, Still opened
six years ago under the creative eye of
Sophia Mason. Being relatively
unknown and slightly tucked away,
there is a high possibility of finding a
great piece here. The staff are very
friendly and the store's pared-down
design means easy shopping. The
décor is minimalist but the ambience
is warm. This was one of the first
stores that cottoned on to the less-is-
more school of thought, which was
previously unheard of on the vintage
scene. Clothes and accessories are
displayed in a 'boutique' style. Best for
early Pucci and Zandra Rhodes, as
well as vintage furs at great prices.
The very inviting open door means
that passers-by walk in out of pure

curiosity. Loved by the fashion
industry and people who like clothes
that have a whisper of vintage about
them rather than those that make an
obvious and over-the-top statement. If
your key thrill is in the 'rummage'
aspect of vintage shopping, you might
be better off going elsewhere. Prices
are pretty reasonable, starting at £45
for a Fifties' dress of an unknown
designer while a Seventies' hand-
painted fully beaded dress by Zandra
Rhodes was on sale for £700.

—Manchester

Origins at Oxfam
Oldham Street, Manchester M1 1JR,
City Centre, Manchester
+44 (0)161 839 3160

Pop Boutique
34 Oldham Street Manchester M1,
City Centre, Manchester
+44 (0)161 236 5797
www.pop-boutique.com

Harriet Appleby
30 Clothorn Road, Didsbury,
Manchester M20 6BP

Bell Antiques
43 Overdale, Swinton, Manchester
M27 5PH
+44 (0)161 728 4911

—Newcastle

Attica
*2 Old George Yard Cloth Market,
Newcastle*
+44 (0)191 261 4062

The Period Clothing Warehouse
*40 Grainger Street, City Centre,
Newcastle-upon-Tyne NE1 5JG*
+44 (0)191 232 5519

—Oxford

Bead Games
40 Cowley Road, Littlemore, Oxford
+44 (0)1865 251 620

**Casa Blanca Costumes at Park End
Antiques & Interiors**
10 Park End Street, Oxford OX1 1HH
+44 (0)1865 200 091

Uncle Sam's
*25 Little Clarendon Street, Jericho,
Oxford OX1 2HU*
+44 (0)1865 510759

—Penzance

Kitt's Couture
*51 Chapel Street, Penzance
TR18 4AF*
+44 (0)1736 350 240
www.kittscouture.co.uk

—Plymouth

Yesterdaze
*18 Southside Street, The Barbican,
Plymouth PL1 2LB*
+44 (0)1752 256 845

—Sheffield

Freshman's Vintage Clothing
6–8 Carver Street, Sheffield S1 4FS
+44 (0)114 272 8333
www.freshmans.co.uk

—Shipley

Era
1 Victoria Road, Saltaire, Shipley
+44 (0)1274 598 777

—Swindon

Agent 69
81 Victoria Road, Swindon SN1 3BB
+44 (0)1793 511 019

—Tideford

Happy Days
Cutcrew, Sawmill, Tideford PL12 5JS
+44 (0)1752 851 402

DIRECTORY

—Todmorden

Echoes
650a Halifax Road, Todmorden
OL14 6DW
+44 (0)1706 817 505

—York

*Priestley's Vintage Clothing
1 Norman Court, 11 Grape Lane,
York YO1 7HU
+44 (0)1904 623 114
Priestley's is a long-established, popular vintage shop in York. Great finds include elegant Thirties' dresses, Forties' cardigans and a selection of lingerie from the turn of the century. Also stocks an impressive range of accessories and menswear. Mid range prices. Credit cards are not accepted.

Wales

—Cardiff

Dax Clothing at Cardiff Antiques Centre
10–12 Royal Arcade, Cardiff
CF10 1AE
+44 (0)29 2039 8891

I Claudius Clothing
8 Castle Arcade, Cardiff CF10 1BU
+44 (0)29 2022 2215

Scotland

—Edinburgh

Armstrongs
83 Grassmarket, Old Town,
Edinburgh EH1 2HJ
+44 (0)131 220 5557
www.armstrongsvintage.co.uk

Flip of Hollywood
59–61 South Bridge, Old Town,
Edinburgh EH1 1LS
+44 (0)131 556 4966

The Grassmarket
15 The Grassmarket, Old Town,
Edinburgh EH1 2HS
+44 (0)131 226 3087

Herman Brown
151 West Port, Edinburgh EH3 9DP
+44 (0)131 228 2589

The Rusty Zip
14 Teviot Place, Edinburgh EH1 2HJ
+44 (0)131 226 4634

—Glasgow

Flip
15 Bath Street, Glasgow G2 1HY
+44 (0)141 204 1846

Glory Hole
41 Ruthven Lane, Byres Road,
West End, Glasgow G12 9BG
+44 (0)141 357 5662

Mr Ben
Unit 6, King's Court, 99 King Street,
Glasgow G1 5RB
+44 (0)141 553 1936

Nicol's Originals
8 Chancellor Street, West End,
Glasgow G11 5Q
+44 (0)141 337 6994

Retro
8 Otago Street, Kelvinbridge,
Glasgow G12 8JH
+44 (0)141 576 0165
www.retro-clothes.com

Saratoga Trunk
Unit 10, 61 Hydepark Street,
Glasgow G3 8BW
+44 (0)141 221 4433

Starry Starry Nights
19–21 Dowanside Lane, Byres Road,
West End, Glasgow G12 9BZ
+44 (0)141 337 1837

Trip
Unit 4, King's Court, 107 King
Street, Glasgow G1 5RA
+44 (0)141 553 1777

Ireland

—Belfast

Rusty Zip
28 Botanic Avenue, Belfast BT7 1JK
+44 (0)28 9024 9700

—Cork

Hale Bop
22 Paul Street, Cork
+353 (0)21 434 5302

—Dublin

A store is born
34 Clarendon Street, Dublin 2 IE
+353 (0)1 679 5866

Big Whiskey
Market Arcade, Dublin 2 IE
+353 (0)1 677 9299

Damascus
2 Crown Alley, Dublin 2 IE
+353 (0)1 679 7087

Flip
4 Upper Fownes Street, Dublin 2 IE
+353 (0)1 671 4299

Harlequin
13 Castle Market, Dublin 2 IE
+353 (0)1 671 0202

Jenny Vander
20 Market Arcade, George's Street,
Dublin 2 IE
+353 (0)1 677 0406
Jenny Vander – the most famous name
on the vintage scene in Ireland – has
long been popular with fashionistas all
over the country as well as those further
afield. Specialises in Fifties' fashion and
stocks a vast range of costume jewellery
in near perfect condition. Provides
costumes to the TV industry.

SeSi
13 Temple Bar Square, Temple Bar,
Dublin 2 IE
+353 (0)1 679 0523

US

—Alabama

Upstairs Style
120 North College Street, Auburn, AL
+1 334 887 2207

Mountain Top Flea Market
11301 US Highway 278W, Attalla, AL
+1 205 589 2706
www.mountaintopfleamarket.com

Bessemer Flea Market
1013 8th Avenue North, Bessemer, AL
+1 205 425 8510

Birmingham Fairgrounds Flea Market
Alabama State Fairgrounds,
Birmingham, AL
+1 205 822 3348

450 Mile Market
Highway 127, Gadsden, AL
+1 205 549 0391

Huntsville Flea Market
Memorial Parkway, Huntsville, AL
+1 800 672 8988

Once Upon a Time
1576 Ann Street, Montgomery, AL
+1 334 834 5515

—Alaska

Rage Vintage Clothing
1936 East 7th Avenue, Anchorage
AK 99501
+1 907 274 7243

—Arizona

Wardrobe Costume & Vintage
920 North Broad Street, Globe,
AZ 85501
+1 928 425 7974

Yesterdaze Wearables
2413 East Osborn Road, Phoenix,
AZ 85016
+1 602 957 3944

Gigi's Second Time Around
7126 East Becker Lane, Scottsdale,
AZ 85254
+1 480 998 5978

Desert Vintage & Costume
636 North 4th Avenue, Tuscon,
AZ 85705
+1 520 620 1570

How Sweet it Was
419 North 4th Avenue, Tuscon,
AZ 85705
+1 520 623 9854

—Arkansas

Soho Vintage
906 Front Street, Conway, AR
+1 501 336 0200

Threads
821 West Faulkner Street,
El Dorado, AR
+1 870 862 8146

Something for Everyone
614 Sycamore, Suite C, Fayetteville,
AR 72703
+1 501 444 9881

Private Treasures by Etta
701 Parkdale Street, Little Rock, AR
+1 501 945 5314

—California

Alameda Antiques & Teas
1519 Park Street, Alameda, CA
+1 510 814 8014

Victorian Closet
14176 Highway 49, Amador City,
CA 95601
+1 209 267 5250
www.antique-adventures.com

Lily et Cie

Where? 9044 Burton Way, Beverly Hills, CA 90211
+1 310 724 5757

Why go there? This store is said to stock the largest selection of museum-quality pieces in the whole of the US. It has all of Madame Grès's original samples and boasts the world's largest collection of Rudi Gernreich pieces, as well as other key pieces by Norell, Yves Saint Laurent, Balenciaga, Givenchy, Trigère.

What's it like? The entrance to the store is very unassuming. Once you get inside, however, it is like being in a very prestigious museum. The floor and walls are bare concrete, Art Deco-style rails hold pristine vintage pieces lined up in a very orderly fashion while the owner Rita Watnick sits at a desk at the end of the large room. Very intimidating.

Best for? Very high-end couture.

Clientele? Celebrities – Renée Zellwegger, Kate Moss, Demi Moore – stylists, collectors, designers and curators.

Hot tip? If you are looking for a bargain, forget it. The same goes for the easily intimidated. This store is for serious buyers only. Also, Watnick's small dog, Trouble, has free run of the store so if you don't like canines – no matter how cute and friendly – it's probably better to shop elsewhere.

Prices? Starts from $400. After that, the sky is the limit. Note, all prices are upon application.

Polkadots Costume & Vintage
Clothing
207 South 1st Street, Arcadia, CA

Maggies Vintage Clothing
1121 High Street, Auburn, CA
95603
+1 530 888 0988

Those Were the Days
1586 Lincoln Way, Auburn,
CA 95603
+1 530 823 2519

Grandma's Trunk
1115 H Street, Bakersfield, CA
+1 661 323 2730

Discover Yesterday
364 First Street, Benicia, CA
+1 707 747 0726

Mars Mercantile
2398 Telegraph Avenue, Berkeley,
CA 94704
+1 510 843 6711

Sharks
2505 Telegraph Avenue, Berkeley, CA
+1 510 841 8736

Stop the Clock
2110 Addison Street, Berkeley,
CA 94704
+1 510 841 2142

Time Zone Vintage Clothing
2447 San Pablo Avenue, Berkeley, CA
+1 510 843 4645

Twisters Vintage
2500 San Pablo Avenue, Berkeley, CA
+1 510 548 9478

Fifi's Vintage Clothing
41348 Big Bear Boulevard, Suite 2,
Big Bear Lake, CA 92315

Hubba Bubba
3220 West Magnolia Boulevard
Burbank, CA 91505
+1 818 845 0636

Audrey's Antiques
1208 Donnelly Avenue, Burlingame,
CA 94010
+1 650 558 0885

Leanora's Closet
1139 Lincoln Avenue, Calistoga,
CA 94515
+1 752 942 0688

DIRECTORY

23 Skidoo
342 East Campbell Avenue,
Campbell, CA 95008
+1 408 370 2334

Collectible Glitz – Miss la-deda's
21435 Sherman Way, Canoga Park,
CA 91303
+1 818 347 9343

Yesterdays
536 5th Street, Clovis, CA 93612
+1 559 322 9622

Hollyvogue Vintage Clothing
2588 Newport Boulevard, Suite A
Costa Mesa, CA
+1 949 646 4223

Vintage Dreams
132 North Citrus Avenue, Covina, CA
+1 626 339 2000

Vintage Silhouettes
1301 Pomona Street, Crockett,
CA 94525
+1 510 787 7274
www.vintagesilhouettes.com

Flashback
116 West Wabash Avenue, Eureka,
CA 95501
+1 707 268 0855

Mendocino Vintage
300 North Franklin Street, Fort
Bragg, CA 95437
+1 707 964 5825

Fellini's Vintage Clothes
836 North Fulton Street, Fresno,
CA 93728
+1 559 498 3321

Retro Rag
733 East Olive Avenue, Fresno,
CA 93728
+1 559 497 0717

Geez Louise
101 East Commonwealth Avenue
Fullerton, CA 93832
+1 714 871 4375

Out of Vogue
109 East Commonwealth Avenue
Fullerton, CA 93832
+1 714 879 6647

Stray Cat Vintage & Costume
108 North Harbor Boulevard,
Fullerton, CA 92832
+1 714 738 5680

Glory Days Vintage Clothing
14301 Arnold Drive, Glen Ellen,
CA 95442
+1 707 935 3305

Glorious Old Clothes
107 West Main Street, Grass Valley,
CA 95945
+1 530 477 9001

Granny Takes a Trip
1411 Hermosa Avenue, Hermosa
Beach, CA
+1 310 318 6442

Treasure Chest
50 Pier Avenue, Hermosa Beach, CA
+1 310 372 5644

Lundberg Haberdashery
396 Colusa Avenue, Kensington,
CA 94707
+1 510 524 3003

Tamara's Vieux Carre
333 South Coast Highway, Laguna
Beach, CA 92651
+1 949 497 4332

Bubbly Hills
4354 Atlantic Avenue, Long Beach,
CA 90807
+1 562 997 7939

Little Treasures at Antiques & More
327 Pine Avenue, Long Beach,
CA 90802
+1 562 598 1423

MEOW
2210 East 4th Street, Long Beach,
CA 90814
+1 562 438 8990

Steel Magnolias Antiques
832 La Mesa Boulevard, La Mesa,
CA 91941
+1 619 469 2832

Cherry West
8250 Santa Monica Boulevard,
West Hollywood, Los Angeles, CA
+1 323 650 4698

Come to Mama
4019 West Sunset Boulevard, Los
Angeles, CA 90029
+1 323 953 1275

Decades
8214 Melrose Venue, Los Angeles,
CA 90046
+1 323 655 0223

Entre Nous
8430 West 3rd Street, Los Angeles,
CA
+1 323 655 9096

Gollyester Antiques
136 South La Brea Avenue,
Los Angeles, CA 90036
+1 323 931 1339

I like **Doris Raymond's shop in LA, The Way We Wore**. *She has the most exquisite taste. Things that have a historic significance are always collectables. It is so interesting to acquire vintage pieces that tell a story of our history.*

ZAC POSEN
Fashion designer

The Way We Wore

Where? 334 South La Brea Avenue, Los Angeles, CA 90036
+1 323 937 0878

Why go there? Whether you're looking for an everyday vintage piece or a haute couture gown, you will not be disappointed. Everything in this store looks handpicked and is in fantastic quality. Very friendly owner Doris Raymond runs the store with equally pleasant staff.

What's it like? Stepping into The Way We Wore is like visiting a huge walk-in wardrobe in a fashionistas's padded cell. Yes, the walls are white patent and padded. Look up and the ceiling is made up of a dramatic gold metallic canopy. Look down and the flooring is a leopard print carpet. Downstairs is crammed full of accessories, and clothing right from the nineteenth century to 1980s. The upper floor on the other hand is dedicated to incredible haute couture pieces. Considering this shop stocks such exquisite pieces, it has a very relaxed ambience.

Best for? Couture. Pieces from Givenchy, Charles James, Balenciaga, Pucci, Rudi Gernreich, Grès... this list goes on. Also has an extensive range of jewellery.

Clientele? Celebrities such as Winona Ryder and Lenny Kravitz, contemporary designers such as John Galliano looking for inspiration, museum curators, chic 'ladies who lunch', costume jewellery aficionados.

Hot tip? Opens everyday with the exception of Monday, which is by appointment only. The owner keeps a huge stock of fragile couture pieces away from the shop floor. If you are looking for something in particular, you can set up an appointment to view this collection.

Prices? Very varied. A Forties' tea dress without a label can cost $65 whereas if you go upstairs to the haute couture section you can spend anything from $400 to $20,000.

DIRECTORY

Kimono-Ya
*10800 West Pico Boulevard,
Suite 135, Los Angeles, CA 90064*
+1 310 475 8789

Kimono-Ya
*10250 Santa Monica Boulevard,
Suite 440, Los Angeles, CA 90067*
+1 310 286 1121

Jet Rag
*1001 East 62nd Street, Los Angeles,
CA 90001*
+1 323 232 1191

Julian Vintage Clothing
*8366 West 3rd Street, Los Angeles,
CA 90048*
+1 323 655 3011

Paper Bag Princess
*8700 Santa Monica Boulevard,
Los Angeles, CA 90069*
+1 310 358 1985

Polkadots & Moonbeam
*8367 West 3rd Street, Los Angeles,
CA*
+1 323 651 1746

Pull My Daisy
*3908 West Sunset Boulevard,
Los Angeles, CA 90029*
+1 323 663 0608

Resurrection
*8006 Melrose Avenue, Los Angeles,
CA 90046*
+1 323 651 5516

Shabon
*7617 West Beverly Boulevard,
Los Angeles, CA 90036*
+1 323 692 0061

Star Shoes
*6364 Hollywood Boulevard,
Los Angeles, CA 90028*
+1 323 462 7827
This unique store is adored by shoe addicts and bar hoppers alike. The dimly lit cocktail bar, frequented by the starry Hollywood crowd, doubles up as a shoe store that occasionally holds exhibitions showing the work of Californian artists. The shoes on sale are original never-been-worn designs by Joseph LaRose who made shoes for the likes of Jayne Mansfield and Betty Grable. Stored in glass cases, some of these exquisite creations date back to the Forties. If you'd rather spend your cash on cocktails than a pair of $200 shoes, you can get your own shoes shined for a mere $5. However, lets face it, where else can you have the pleasure of simultaneously sipping a martini and buying amazing shoes at such an ungodly hour?

Camille's Vintage Clothing
1000 Clinton, Napa, CA 94559-
2546
+1 510 255 8791

Gloria's Place
23123 West Lyons Avenue, Newhall,
CA 91321
+1 661 254 0671

Age of Innocence
11054 Magnolia Boulevard, North
Hollywood (NOHO), CA 91601
+1 818 980 0462

Alice & Annie
11056 Magnolia Boulevard, North
Hollywood (NOHO), CA 91601
+1 818 761 6085

Kathy's E Boutique
11114 Magnolia Boulevard, North
Hollywood (NOHO), CA 91601
+1 818 505 0035

Playclothes Vintage Fashions
11422 Moorpark Street, North
Hollywood (NOHO), CA 91602
+1 818 755 9559

Madame Butterfly
5474 College Avenue, Oakland,
CA 94618
+1 510 653 1525

Attic Delights
138 South Glasell Street, Orange,
CA 92866
+1 714 639 8351

Flashbacks Vintage Clothing
465 North Tustin Avenue, Orange,
CA 92867
+1 714 771 4912

Karla's Antiques
83 Orinda Way, Orinda, CA
+1 510 254 0964

Reincarnation Vintage Clothing
214 17th Street, Pacific Grove,
CA 93950
+1 831 649 0689

1860–1960
15266 Antioch Street, Pacific
Palisades, CA 90272
+1 310 459 4114

Trappings of Time
470 Hamilton Avenue, Palo Alto,
CA 94301
+1 630 323 3061

Rebecca's Dream Inc
16 South Fair Oaks Avenue,
Pasadena, CA 91105
+1 626 796 1204

DIRECTORY

Empress
583 Main Street, Placerville, CA
+1 530 642 2555

Vintage Clothing
Adobe Kottinger Barn, 200 Ray Street, Pleasanton, CA
+1 925 417 7440

Fine Vintage
2629 Aramon Drive, Rancho Cardova, CA 95670
+1 916 369 6513

Roseville Antique Mall
238 Vernon Street, Roseville, CA 95678
+1 916 773 4003

Cheap Thrills
1217 21st Street, Sacramento, CA 95814
+1 916 446 1366

Prevues Clothing
2417 K Street, Sacramento, CA 95816
+1 916 448 4556

Renaissance The Designer Consignor
2362 Fair Oaks Boulevard, Sacramento, CA 95825
+1 916 485 4911

Vintage Flamingo
528 San Anselmo Avenue, San Anselmo, CA 94960
+1 415 721 7275

Cherry Pickers Vintage Clothing
4230 Adams Avenue, San Diego, CA 92116
+1 619 281 2821

Daze of Future Past
4879 Newport Avenue, San Diego, CA 92107
+1 619 222 0220

Flashbacks
3847 5th Avenue, San Diego, CA 92103
+1 619 291 4200

Life's Little Pleasures
4219 Park Boulevard, San Diego, CA 92103
+1 619 296 6222

Memories Boutique
1916 Cable Street, San Diego, CA 92107
+1 619 224 8828

Shake Rag – Epicenter
440 F Street, San Diego, CA 92101
+1 619 237 4955

Wearing It Again Sam
3922 Park Boulevard, San Diego,
CA 92103
+1 619 299 0185

What Ever
6495 El Cajon Boulevard,
San Diego, CA 92115
+1 619 582 2006

560 Hayes
560 Hayes Street, San Francisco,
CA 94102
+1 415 861 7993

Aardvark Odd Ark
1501 Haight Street, San Francisco,
CA 94117
+1 415 621 3141

Arc of San Francisco
2101 Mission Street, San Francisco,
CA
+1 415 626 5710

Captain Jacks
866 Valencia Street, San Francisco,
CA 94110
+1 415 648 1065

Cookies Closet
1094a 38 Revere Street,
San Francisco, CA 94102
+1 415 970 50730

Departures from the Past
2028 Fillmore Street, San Francisco,
CA 94115
+1 415 885 3377

Guys & Dolls Vintage
3789 24th Street, San Francisco, CA
+1 415 285 7174

Held Over
1543 Haight Street, San Francisco,
CA 94117
+1 415 864 0818

La Rosa
1711 Haight Street, San Francisco,
CA 94117
+1 415 668 3744

Leopard Room
1825 Polk Street, San Francisco, CA
+1 415 923 0175

Martini Mercantile
1773 Haight Street, San Francisco,
CA 94117
+1 415 668 3746

Nellus Antique
357 Miller Avenue, San Francisco, CA
+1 415 388 2277

DIRECTORY

Old Vogue
1412 Grant Avenue, San Francisco,
CA 94133
+1 415 392 1522

Retro-Fit Vintage
910 Valencia Street, San Francisco,
CA 94110
+1 415 550 1530

Satellite Vintage
1364 Haight Street, San Francisco,
CA 94117
+1 415 626 1364

Schauplatz
791 Valencia Street, San Francisco,
CA 94110
+1 415 864 5665

Third Hand
1839 Divisadero Street,
San Francisco, CA
+1 415 567 7332

Wasteland
1660 Haight Street, San Francisco,
CA 94117
+1 415 863 3150

Ver Unica
437b Haight Street, San Francisco,
CA 94114
+1 415 431 0688

Moon Zoom
1630 West San Carlos, San Jose,
CA 94070
+1 408 287 5876

Park Place
1318 Lincoln Avenue, San Jose,
CA 95125

Decades
785 Higuera Street, San Luis
Obispo, CA 93401
+1 805 546 0901

Come C
159 South Boulevard, San Mateo,
CA 94402
+1 650 571 8084

Deja Nu
1224 4th Street, San Rafael,
CA 94901
+1 415 258 0200

Santa Barbara Vintage Clothing
519 Chiquita Road, Santa Barbara,
CA 93101
+1 805 962 9322

Victorian Vogue
1224 State Street, Santa Barbara,
CA 93101
+1 805 962 8824

Love Me 2 Times
1331 Mission Street, Santa Cruz,
CA 95060
+1 831 429 6210

Rage
1349 Pacific Avenue, Santa Cruz, CA

Seek & Find Vintage Collection
853 41st Avenue, Santa Cruz,
CA 95062
+1 831 477 1497

Victoria's Vintage Clothing
428 Front Street, Santa Cruz,
CA 95060
+1 831 457 9262

BBC Vintage Clothing
517 Santa Monica Boulevard,
Santa Monica, CA
+1 310 395 1300

The Finery/Vintage Vintage
1611 Montana Avenue, Santa
Monica, CA 90403
+1 310 393 5588

Kimono-Ya
Santa Monica Place, Suite 281,
Santa Monica, CA 90401
+1 310 458 7738

Paris 1900
2703 Main Street, Santa Monica,
CA 90405
+1 310 396 0405

Snap Vintage Clothing
3211 Pico Boulevard, Santa Monica,
CA
+1 310 453 4177

Wednesday's House
2409 Main Street, Santa Monica,
CA 90405
+1 310 452 4486

Hot Couture
101 3rd Street, Santa Rosa,
CA 95401
+1 707 528 7247

The Antique Society
2661 Gravenstein Highway, South
Sebastopol, Sebostopol, CA 95472
+1 707 829 1733

School Bell Antiques
3555 Gravenstein Highway, South
Sebastopol, Sebostopol, CA 95472
+1 707 823 2878

She Wore Blue Velvet
207 North Main Street, Sebastopol,
CA 95472
+1 707 823 6015

DIRECTORY

Cranberry House
12318 Ventura Boulevard,
Studio City, CA 91604
+1 818 506 8945

Hidden Treasures
154 South Topanga Canyon
Boulevard, Topanga, CA 90290
+1 310 455 2998

Animal House
66 Windward Avenue, Venice,
CA 90291
+1 310 392 5411

Ventura
Old Hat Vintage Clothing, 56 South
Oak Street, Ventura, CA 93001
+1 805 653 7220

—Colorado

Candy's Vintage Clothing
4483 Broadway Street, Boulder,
CO 80304
+1 303 442 6186
www.candysvintageclothing.com

Classic Facets
942 Pearl Street, Boulder, CO
+1 303 938 8851

Counter Evolution
1628 Pearl Street, Boulder,
CO 80302
+1 303 444 1799

The Ritz
959 Walnut Street, Boulder,
CO 80302
+1 303 443 2850

My Mother's Attic Antiques
6660 Delmonico Drive, Suite 405
Colorado Springs, CO 80919
+1 719 528 2594

Repeat Performance
829 North Union Boulevard,
Colorado Springs, CO 80909
+1 719 633 1325

Rev 2
403 North Tejon Street, Colorado
Springs, CO 80903
+1 719 635 4944

A Celebrity Vintage Clothing
1866 S Broadway, Denver, CO
80210-3104
+1 303 778 2385

Five & Dime 13th Avenue
606 East 13th Avenue, Denver,
CO 80203-2613
+1 303 861 4979

Miami Twice

Where? 6562 Bird Road / 6562 Southwest 40th Street, Miami, FL 33155-4830 +1 305 666 0127

Why go there? It is the most famous vintage shop in Miami and has won best vintage store accolade many times over. The fact that it is so unusually large for an antique clothing store makes it worth seeing.

What's it like? For such a well-known store, Miami Twice resides in an inconspicuous area. Hemmed in between two anonymous looking shops, it is the diamond in the rough. This emporium is run by Diana Kyle and her two daughters. It is absolutely huge – 5,000 square feet to be exact – filled with clothing and accessories spanning every decade. It features amazing pieces from Givenchy, Pucci, Trigère and Pierre Cardin as well as an extensive selection of Yves Saint Laurent shoes. For those who aren't necessarily interested in designer names, it offers a selection of beautiful pieces from no-name labels with price points as low as $35. Hat lovers should be prepared. The artistic and elaborate wall display of headpieces is not to be missed. Miami Twice also carries a large range of antique furniture that goes as far back as the 1800s.

Best for? Yves Saint Laurent shoes, mint condition Seventies' evening dresses, Sixties' mini dresses and hats.

Clientele? Designers, journalists and anyone looking for a 'wow' party outfit. Furniture enthusiasts are also quite common.

Hot tip? To get a true indication of their stock, avoid visiting between the end of August and the end of October. During these months, Miami Twice is completely transformed into a fancy dress emporium for Hallowe'en devotees and the vintage key pieces are put into storage.

Prices? Pucci pieces start from $600 and rise up to $2,500. Yves Saint Laurent shoes start from $75 while a striking gold, full-length Grecian dress is a very reasonable $49.

Sasparilla

Where? 1630 Pennsylvania Avenue (just off Lincoln Road), Miami Beach, FL 33139
+1 305 532 6611

Why go there? Owners Ken Harvey and Ronnie Lewis, ex NYC fashion insiders, have sold to every celebrity stylist and most American designers. Epitomises the adage about beautiful things coming in small packages.

What's it like? Small and intimate, Sasparilla is like a friend's living room, albeit a super sylish friend: comfy sofa, copies of *Vogue*, 1961 *Harpers Bazaar* poster and a glass-encased Pucci jacket. The 'bookcase' displays are accessorised with bags, shoes and belts. There is a clever mix of carefully selected new labels such as Miu Miu, Marc Jacobs and Fendi and vintage goodies from Courrèges, Charles Jourdan and Giorgio di Sant'Angelo. In addition, there is striking 'Award Ceremony' worthy jewellery. One piece in particular – a sapphire and diamante bracelet and earring set – caught the eye of revered American designer Bill Blass, so much so that he requested the use of these pieces for his catwalk show.

Best for? Rare Charles Jourdan shoes, vintage jewellery, eveningwear and key pieces from recent collections of contemporary designers

Clientele? Fashion stylists, Kate Moss, Lenny Kravitz and Sheryl Crow. The staff are extremely friendly and welcome people of all ages and from walks of life; the client base ranges from early 20s to late 50s.

Hot tip? If you are looking for a specific style or designer that you can't see out on the racks, ask the staff. Sasparilla offer private sales, but they keep a lot of their couture/one-off pieces at their branch in Atlanta.

Prices? Lower-end price points are rarities, such as an autumnal pussy-bow dress at $65 and a Kenneth Jay Lane jade ring on sale for $95. Most pieces go from $200 upwards – a Seventies' snakeskin bag costs $200 and the jewellery set Bill Blass fell in love with is $250. Couture pieces like a Fifties' sequinned dress start from a pocket-stretching $1,800.

Bloomingdeals
2512 Williams Street, Denver,
CO 80205-5526
+1 303 831 9505

Boss Unlimited
18 South Broadway, Denver,
CO 80203
+1 303 871 0373

Flossy McGrews
1959 South Broadway, Denver,
CO 80210
+1 308 778 0853

Irene's
2342 South Colorado Boulevard,
Denver, CO 80222
+1 303 759 3010

Soul Flower
114 South Broadway, Denver,
CO 80209
+1 303 778 7823

Indigo Rose
220 Linden Street, Fort Collins,
CO 80524
+1 970 482 3449

My Groovy Closet
170 North College Avenue,
Fort Collins, CO 80524
+1 970 482 1778

Common Era 2000
1500 Pearl Street, Sterling,
CO 80571
+1 970 521 0828

—Connecticut

Sophia's Great Dames
1 Liberty Way, Greenwich, CT 06830
+1 203 869 5990

Retro Active
58 River Street, Milford, CT 06460
+1 203 877 6050

Petria Boutiq
Route 44, Norfolk, CT
+1 860 542 5511
www.petriaboutiq.com

Crystal Valentine
56 Main Street, Norwalk, CT 06854
+1 203 853 4727

Burke & Company
13 Bailey, Ridgeway, CT
+1 203 438 2742

Roxie Taylor
39 East Weatogue, Simsbury,
CT 06070
+1 203 658 5141

DIRECTORY

Stratford Antiques Centre
400 Honeyspot Road, Stratford,
CT 06616
+1 203 378 7754

Fannie Rose Vintage Clothing
737 Main Street, Watertown, CT
+1 860 758 6848

—Delaware

Millsboro Bazaar
238 Main Street, Delaware, DE
+1 302 934 7413

Tempest Fugit
149 Rehoboth Avenue, Rehoboth
Beach, Delaware, DE
+1 302 227 1228

Eclectica
1825 Delaware Avenue, Wilmington
Delaware, DE
+1 302 888 1824

Wilmington Trumpets
1903 Delaware Avenue, Wilmington
Delaware, DE 19806
+1 302 425 3636

—Florida

That Was Then
3262 West Hillsboro Boulevard,
Deerfield Beach, FL
+1 954 428 5858

Bonnie's Vintage Emporium
1937 Suwanee Avenue, Fort Meyers,
FL 33901
+1 941 936 4888

Lucky Seven Vintage
12 East University Avenue,
Gainesville, FL 32601
+1 352 374 6864

Persona Vintage Clothing
1023 West University Avenue
Gainesville, FL 32601
+1 352 372 0455

Vintage City
404 North West 10th Avenue
Gainesville, FL
+1 352 375 0800

Looking Glass Cottage Boutique
1558 South Wickham Road,
Melbourne, FL
+1 407 724 5011

Fly Boutique
650 Lincoln Road, Miami Beach,
FL 33139
+1 305 604 8508

Smiley's Antique Mall
17020 County Road 234, Micanopy,
FL 32667
+1 352 466 0707

Antique Addict Vintage Shoppe
180 Race Track Road, Oldsmar,
FL 34677
+1 813 855 9752

DeJa Vu Vintage Clothing
1825 North Orange Avenue,
Orlando, FL 32804
+1 407 898 3609

Orlando Vintage Clothing
2117 W Fairbanks Ave, Winter Park
Orlando, FL 32789-4507
+1 407 599 7225

Collectamania
306 Harrison Avenue, Panama City,
FL 32401
+1 850 913 6173

Years A Go-Go
4165 Barrancas Avenue, Pensacola,
FL
+1 850 458 9777

The Old Lace & Linen Shop
1841 SW 67th Avenue, Plantation,
FL
+1 954 258 2274
www.antiquelinen.com

Volta Clothing
407 West 1st Street, Sanford,
FL 32771
+1 407 323 6992

Creative Collections
527 South Pineapple Avenue,
Sarasota, FL 34236
+1 941 951 0477

Sanders Antiques
22 North Lemon Avenue, Sarasota,
FL 34236
+1 941 366 0400

Tenth Street Antiques
183 10th Street, South Naples, FL
+1 941 649 0323

La France
1612 East 7th Avenue, Tampa,
FL 33605
+1 813 248 1381

Yesterdaze Sherry's Vintage Clothing
& Antiques
1908 South Macdill Avenue, Tampa,
FL 33629
+1 813 258 2388

DIRECTORY

—Georgia

Aunt Teeks
*1166 Euclid Avenue, Northeast
Atlanta, Atlanta, GA
+1 404 525 0630*

Cats Meow
*672 Highland Avenue NE, Atlanta,
GA 30312
+1 404 522 3774*

Dakota J's
*1030 North Highland Avenue,
Atlanta, GA 30306
+1 404 870 0690*

Dressing Room
*504 Flat Shoals Avenue SE, Atlanta,
GA 30316
+1 404 584 2200*

Frocks of Ages
*1653 McLendon Avenue, Atlanta,
GA 30307
+1 404 370 1006*

Groovy Girls
*211 Moreland Avenue, Atlanta, GA
+1 404 659 3669*

The Junkman's Daughter
*1130 Euclid Avenue, Atlanta, GA
+1 404 577 3188*

Stefan's Vintage Clothing
*1160 Euclid Avenue, Atlanta, GA
+1 404 688 4929*

Trashy Diva
*1052 Saint Charles Avenue, Atlanta,
GA 30306
+1 404 872 5040*

Vintage Diva
*3085 East Point Street, Atlanta,
GA 30344
+1 404 767 6575*

Grandmother's Earth
*6229-C Fairburn Road, Douglasville,
GA 30388
+1 770 489 5999*

Twice as Nice Vintage Clothing
*567 North Central Avenue,
Hapeville, GA 3035
+1 404 761 9582*

Aimee's
*168 Roswell Street, Marietta,
GA 30060
+1 770 425 1070*

Moondance Vintage Clothing
*202 Mallory Street, Saint Simmons
Island, GA 31522
+1 912 638 0850*

Faith Hope & Love
415 Whitaker Street, Savannah,
GA 31401
+1 912 234 4673

My Sister's Closet Boutique
5350 Peachtree Road, Chamblee
Savannah, GA 30341
+1 770 458 8362

—Hawaii

Bailey's Antiques & Aloha Shirts
517 Kapahulu Avenue, Honolulu,
HI 96815
+1 808 734 7628

Jan's Secret Closet
3427 A Waialae Avenue, Honolulu,
HI 96816
+1 808 739 1774

Linda's Vintage Isle in Waikiki
2139 Kuhio Avenue, Suite 10
Honolulu, HI 96815
+1 808 921 0430

Linda's Vintage Isle in Waikiki
2909 Waialae Avenue, Suite 44,
Honolulu, HI 96816
+1 808 734 6163

Peggy's Picks
732 Kapahulu Avenue, Suite 1,
Honolulu, HI 96815
+1 808 737 3297

Rockets Vintage Clothing
2520 Kalakaua Avenue, Honolulu,
HI 96815
+1 808 926 1463

Taylor's Vintage
2113 Kalakaua Avenue, Suite J,
Honolulu, HI 96815
+1 808 926 2222

—Idaho

Acquired Again Antiques
1304 Alturas Street, Boise,
ID 83702
+1 208 338 5929

Chester's Vintage Clothing
1747 Broadway Avenue, Boise,
ID 83706
+1 208 368 0862

Picture Show Retro & Vintage
223 North 5th Street, Boise,
ID 83702
+1 208 344 7278

Treasure Gardens
6521 Ustick Road, Boise, ID 83704
+1 208 323 7717

Vintage Vanities
919 South Fir Street, Jerome,
ID 83338
+1 208 324 3067

Déjà Vu
191 North Main Street, Ketchum,
ID 83340
+1 208 726 1908

—Illinois

Arrow
1452 West Chicago Avenue,
Chicago, IL 60622
+1 312 738 2755

Backseat Betty
1540 North Milwaukee Avenue
Chicago, IL 60622
+1 773 227 2427

Beatnik
3400 North Halsted Street, Chicago,
IL 60657
+1 773 281 6933

Chicago Recycle Shop
5308 North Clark Street, Chicago,
IL 60640
+1 773 878 8525

Couture Club
1971 North Fremont, Chicago, IL
+1 773 244 0917

Hyde N Seek Antiques
5210 South Harper Avenue,
Chicago, IL 60615
+1 773 684 8380

Hubba Hubba
3309 North Clark Street, Chicago,
IL 60657
+1 773 477 1414

Lost Era Antiques
1511 West Howard, Chicago, IL
+1 773 764 7400

Shangri LA
1952 West Roscoe Street, Chicago,
IL 60657
+1 773 348 5090

Silver Moon
3337 Halsted Street, Chicago,
IL 60657
+1 773 883 0222

Vintage Fibre Works
1869 North Damen Avenue,
Chicago, IL 60647
+1 773 862 6070

Wacky Cats
3109 North Lincoln Avenue,
Chicago, IL 60657
+1 773 929 6701

Viva Vintage
1043 Chicago Avenue, Evanston,
IL 60202
+1 847 475 5025

Vintage Adventure
403 11th Street, Rockford,
IL 61104
+1 815 227 1892

Waukegan
129 North Genesee Street,
Waukegan, IL 60085
+1 847 244 3100

—Indiana

Another Time
828 East 64th Street, Indianapolis,
IN 46220
+1 317 255 1277

Broad Ripple Vintage
853 East 65th Street, Indianapolis,
IN 46220
+1 317 251 6731

Nostalgia Nook
6 East Main Street, Knightstown, IN
+1 765 345 5665

It's a Wonderful Life Antique Mall
708 Lincoln Way, LaPorte, IN
+1 219 326 7432

Silver Thread
20 East Main Street, Mooresville,
IN 46158
+1 317 834 6440

—Iowa

Timeless Arts
420 Hawkeye Downs Road,
Southwest Cedar Rapids, IA 52404
+1 319 247 6093

Vintage Blues – Pierce School Mall
2212 East 12th Street, Suite 208,
Davenport, IA 52803
+1 319 323 2552

Atomic Garage Vintage Clothing
Company
129 5th Street, West Des Moines,
IA 50265
+1 515 255 2525

—Kansas

Orange Crate Gallery
3125 Southwest Huntoon Street,
Topeka, KS 66604
+1 785 296 9207

Klassic Line Vintage
923 West Douglas, Wichita,
KS 67213
www.tias.com

DIRECTORY

—Kentucky

Elizabeth Timeless Attire
2050 Frankfort Avenue, Louisville,
KY 40206
+1 502 895 5911

Louisville Antique Mall
900 Goss Avenue, Louisville,
KY 40217
+1 502 635 2852

Past Perfect Vintage Clothing
1529 South 2nd Street, Louisville,
KY 40208
+1 502 636 5152

Auntie M's Vintage Boutique
11601 Main Street, Middletown,
KY 40243
+1 502 254 1426

—Louisiana

Jezebel's Art & Antiques
4610 Magazine Street, New Orleans,
LA 70115
+1 504 895 7784
Jezebel's looks more like a colourful beach hut than a vintage shop. This store, however, based on the antique heavy Magazine Street, is one of the best outlets for costume jewellery in the Southern America. You will find extravagant pieces from Miriam Haskell, Stanley Hagler, Pauline Trigère and Eisenberg and Carnegie. They also carry the odd Twenties' heavily beaded flapper dress, usually in mint condition. A word of advice: if you are at the French Quarter end of Magazine Street, take a bus as it is way too far to walk. Also if you visit during summer, call the store before visiting. Most people are away during this time and many dealers operate their opening hours on an ad hoc basis.

—Maine

Orphan Annies
96 Court Street, Auburn, ME 04210
+1 207 782 0638

Arsenic & Old Lace Antiques
Main Street, Damariscotta,
ME 04543
+1 207 563 1414

Vintage Finery
16 Settlers Way, Orrington,
ME 04474
+1 207 825 4142

Connie's Antiques
206 Lincon Avenue, Rumford,
ME 04275
+1 207 364 3363

Gladrags
South Strong Road, Strong,
ME 04983
+1 207 683 2084

—Maryland

Alanna's Vintage Clothing
1033 South Charles Street,
Baltimore, MD 21230
+1 410 837 2170

Fat Elvis
833 West 36th Street, Baltimore,
MD 21211
+1 410 467 6030

Oh Suzanna Vintage
620 South Broadway, Baltimore,
MD 21231
+1 410 327 1408

Vanessa Vintage Treasures
1132 South Charles Street,
Baltinore, MD 21230
+1 410 752 3224

Vintage Rose
141/2 East Hamilton Street,
Baltimore, MD 21202
+1 410 539 9791

Yesteryear
Cumberland

Denton Station Antiques Mall
Denton

Frederick's Best
307 East 2nd Street, Frederick, MD
+1 301 698 1791

Venus on the Half Shell
151 North Market Street, Frederick,
MD
+1 301 662 6213

Severna Park
Retrofit Vintage Clothing, 820
Ritchie Highway, Severna Park, MD
+1 410 421 5454

Victoria Rose
9 Deckman Court, Silver Spring,
MD 20906

Heart's Desire
7518 East Fullerton Road,
Springfield, VA
+1 703 644 3004

Takoma Underground
7030 Carroll Avenue, Takoma Park,
MD
+1 301 270 0874

DIRECTORY

—Massachusetts

Bobbie from Boston
19 Thayer Street, Boston, MA 02118
+1 617 423 9299

Charles River Street Antiques
45 River Street, Boston, MA 02108
+1 617 367 3244

Closet Upstairs
223 Newbury Street, Boston,
MA 02116
+1 617 267 5757

Warped
236 Elm Street, Boston, MA
+1 617 666 3129

Oona's Experienced Clothing
1210 Massachusetts Avenue,
Cambridge, MA 02138
+1 617 491 2654

Café Society
131 Cypress Street, Brookline, MA
+1 617 738 7186

Clothes Encounters
1394 Beacon Street, Brookline,
MA 02446
+1 617 277 3031

Reddog Vintage Clothing
1076 Cambridge Street, Cambridge,
MA 02139
+1 617 666 1986

Circa Vintage Wear
42 Main Street, Fairhaven,
MA 02719
+1 508 997 9390

Reflections in Vintage Clothing
7 City Hall Avenue, Gardner,
MA 01440
+1 978 630 3710

The Fainting Couch
Mansfield, MA 02048
+1 508 339 7733
faintingcouch@attbi.com

Greystone Gardens
436 North Street, Pittsfield,
MA 01201
+1 413 442 9291

Absolutely Fabulous
108 Beacon Street, Sommerville,
MA 92143
+1 617 864 0656

Davenport & Company
146 Bowdoin Street, Springfield, MA
+1 413 781 1505

Alice Vintage Clothes

Where? 4703 McPherson Avenue, St Louis, MO 63108
+1 314 361 4006

Why go there? Beautiful authentic and very traditional vintage shop.

What's it like? The entrance is extremely quaint. So much so, you could have stepped back in time into your great-grandmother's closet. Romantic Victorian and Edwardian pieces hang from the ceiling and walls, the glass cases hold the most exquisite jewellery from the likes of Miriam Haskell, Robert, Coro and Trifari. The dressing room at the back of the store features a French antique dressing table with a huge oval mirror. The room itself is pale yellow padded silk with a Victorian style canopy. Lingerie of all sorts spill out of antique chest of drawers and top shelves are imaginatively stacked with vintage hatboxes.

Best for? Victorian clothing, lingerie, negligees, costume jewellery and fur coats.

Clientele? Mainly the locals and vintage dealers across America.

Hot tip? If you are buying a few things, enquiring about a discount is perfectly acceptable. Look at for the discounted section where you can pick up a camisole or blouse for as little as $10.

Prices? It's considered one of the more pricey vintage shops in St Louis, however there are bargains to be had. A peach lace Victorian blouse was priced at $28, a 100% cashmere cardigan from the Fifties, $45, and a pair of real croc shoes, $15.

DIRECTORY

Linda White Antique Clothing
2 Maple Avenue, Upton, MA 01568
+1 508 529 4439

—Michigan

Cat's Meow
213 South State Street, Ann Arbor,
MI 48108
+1 734 995 9500

Rage of the Age
314 South Ashley Street, Ann Arbor,
MI 48108
+1 734 662 0777

The Style Revival
110 East Liberty Street, Ann Arbor,
MI 48108

Cinderella's Attic
369 East Maple Road, Birmingham,
MI 48010
+1 248 546 7209

Cadillac
Saturn Gems, 109 North Mitchell
Street, Cadillac, MI 49601
+1 231 876 2040

Retro Image Clothing
14246 Michigan Avenue, Dearborn,
MI
+1 313 582 3074

Beatnix on the Avenue
22751 Woodward Avenue,
Detroit–Ferndale, MI 48220
+1 248 547 9797

Cinderella's Attic
319 West Nine Mile,
Detroit–Ferndale, MI
+1 248 546 7209

The Dandelion Antique Shoppe
114 West 4th Street, Detroit–Royal
Oak, MI
+1 248 547 6288

Detroit Antique Mall
824 West Fisher Freeway,
Detroit–Down Town, MI 48220
+1 313 963 5252

Mother Fletchers
234 West Nine Mile Road,
Detroit–Ferndale, MI 48220
+1 248 398 4816

Showtime Clothing
5708 Woodward Avenue,
Detroit–Down Town, MI 48202
+1 313 875 9280

When I Was A Kid
120 West Hamlin Street, Eaton
Rapids, MI
+1 517 663 5334/1834

Nobody's Sweetheart
*953 Fulton Street, East Grand
Rapids, MI 49503*
+1 616 454 1673

Bird-In-Hand
123 Nagonaba Street, Northport, MI
+1 231 386 7104

Rage of the Age
*3448 Hagadorn Road, Okemos, MI
48864*
+1 517 482 2560

Salt CityAntiques
*116 West Michigan Avenue, Saline,
MI 48176*
+1 734 429 3997

Apple Annies Vintage Clothing
*29 East Cross Street, Ypsilanti, MI
48198*
+1 734 481 0555

—Minneapolis

Elsie's Closet Vintage
*3554 Nicollet Avenue, Twin City,
Minneapolis, MN*
+1 612 825 5627

Gabriela's Vintage Clothing & Jewelry
*1404 West Lake Street, Twin City,
Minneapolis, MN 55408*
+1 612 822 1512

Repeat Performance Vintage
*3404 Lyndale Avenue, South
Minneapolis, MN 55408*
+1 612 824 3035

Roses Vintage
*1330 Grand Avenue, St Paul
Minneapolis, MN 55105*
+1 651 696 5242

Via's Vintage Wear
*2405 Hennepin Avenue,
Minneapolis, MN 55405*
+1 612 374 3649

—Missouri

Deco 2 Moderne
7529 Forsyth, Clayton, MO 63105
+1 314 727 6456

Odile's Vintage Lace & Linens Etc
*34 South Third Street, Sainte
Genevieve, MO 63670*
+1 573 883 2675

Dottie Mae's Collectible Clothing
*7927 Wornall Road, Kansas City,
MO 64114*
+1 816 361 1505

Vintage Vogue Apparel
*4804 Noland Road, Kansas City,
MO 64133*
+1 816 373 7711

DIRECTORY

Demay Furs Limited
*2020 Cherokee Street, Saint Louis,
MO 63108*
+1 314 664 4700

Retro 101 / Pixie 9 Vintage
*2114 Cherokee Street, St Louis,
MO 63118*
+1 314 776 3739
www.pixie9vintage.com
This cool shop – looks more like an old bar – doubles up as a vintage furniture outlet. Retro 101 has some of the best priced vintage in St Louis. While purchasing fur capes – in great condition for as little as $30 – you can also bag yourself a very sought-after kitsch TV from the Fifties. Considering it's a pretty small shop, the range of accessories is extensive and well priced; shoes start from $35.

Rag O Rama
*6388 Delmar Boulevard, St Louis,
MO*
+1 314 725 2760

Remember Me
*1021 Russell Boulevard, Saint Louis,
MO 63104*
+1 314 773 1930

Ruth's Vintage Clothing
2003 Cherokee, St Louis, MO 63118
+1 314 865 1091

Vintage Haberdashery
*3143 South Grand Boulevard, Saint
Louis, MO 63104*
+1 314 772 1927

—Montana

Montana Vintage Clothing
*2509 Montana Avenue, Billings,
MT 59101*
+1 406 248 7650

Take Two Vintage & Collectibles
*2 West Main Street, Bozeman,
MT 59715*
+1 406 586 8324

Rediscoveries Vintage Clothing
55 West Park, Butte, MT
+1 406 723 2176

Karmas Vintage Clothing
Helena, MT 59601
+1 406 442 1159

Grandma's Treasures
*211 South Main Street, Livingston,
MT 59047*
+1 406 222 2177

Mr Higgins Vintage Clothing &
Costume
*612 South Higgins Avenue,
Missoula, MT*
+1 406 721 6446

Red Willow Dry Goods
111 Main Street, Victor, MT 59875
+1 406 642 3130

—Nebraska

Rialto Extra
1725 O Street, Lincoln, NE 68508
+1 402 476 7680

Ruby Begonias
1321 P Street, Lincoln, NE 68508
+1 402 438 4438

Second Chance Antiquities
1116 Jackson Street, Omaha,
NE 68102
+1, 402 346 4930

—Nevada

Revelations
512 North Curry Street, Carson City,
NV 89703
+1 775 882 8950

The Attic
1018 South Main Street, Las Vegas,
NV 89101
+1 702 388 4088

Retro Vintage Store
906 South Valley View Boulevard,
Las Vegas, NV
+1 702 877 8989

Viva Vintage
4800 South Maryland Parkway,
Las Vegas, NV 89119
+1 702 798 8482

Carol Rose Vintage
912 South Virginia Street, Reno,
NV 89506
+1 775 324 1953

Katie Magoo
100 West Pueblo Street, Reno,
NV 89509
+1 775 329 8553

—New Hampshire

Antique Apparel
Acworth, NH 03601
+1 603 835 2295

Kelly Wingate
2 Folsom Road, Centre Osipee,
NH 03814
+1 603 539 6047

Victorian on Main Street
Route 10, Haverhill, NH
+1 603 989 3380

Rainments & Adornments
Colonial Plaza Antiques, West
Lebanon, NH
+1 603 298 8132

The Swan's Bonnet
North Main Street, Wolfeboro,
NH 03894
+ 1603 569 3595

—New Jersey

Nostalgic Nonsense
903 Main Street, Belmar, NJ 07719
+1 732 681 8810

Ellen Christine
668 Washington Street, Cape May,
NJ
+1 609 884 3888

A Place in Time
7 Broadway, Creskill, NJ 07626
+1 201 541 9344

Portabello Road
488 Curry Avenue, Englewood, NJ
+1 201 816 8822

Havenwood's Vintage Corner
58 High Street, Mount Holly, NJ

Via Vai Vintage
12 West Mechanic Street,
New Hope, PA
+1 215 862 6833

Lizzie Tish
Sky Manor Airport, Pittstown, NJ
08867
+1 908 996 1000

Fluffy Ruffles
Point Pleasant Antique Emporium
Bay & Trenton Avenues, Point
Pleasant Beach, NJ
+1 732 892 2222

Charisma 7 Classics
212 Wanaque Avenue, Pompton
Lakes, NJ 07442
+1 973 839 7779

Backward Glances
15 Monmouth Street, Red Bank,
NJ 07701
+1 732 842 9156

Monroe's
12 South Broad Street, Ridgewood,
NJ 07450
+1 201 251 9400

Odds & Adds
Rutherford, NJ
+1 201 438 2485

Incogneeto
93 West Main Street, Sommerville,
NJ 08876
+1 908 722 4600

Revival Vintage
186 Center Avenue, Westwood,
NJ 07675
+1 201 722 9005

—New Mexico

A Few of My Favourite Things
111 Amherst, Albuquerque,
NM 87106
+1 505 254 9600

Barrymore's Vintage Wear
110 Morningside Drive
Southeast Albuquerque, NM 87108

Off Broadway
3110 Central Avenue, Southeast
Albuquerque, NM 87106
+1 505 268 1489

Barbara Rosen Antique & Estate Jewelry
85 West Marcy Street, Santa Fe,
NM 87501
+1 505 992 3000

Fairy Queen's Boutique
316 Garfield Street, Sante Fe,
NM 87501
+1 505 983 4908

Retrospect
1532 Paseo De Pralta, Santa Fe,
NM 87501
+1 505 820 1400

—New York

Daybreak Antique Clothing
22 Central Avenue, Albany, NY
12210
+1 518 434 4312

Lulu's New & Vintage Clothing
Buffalo

Up Your Attic
10255 Main Street, Clarence,
NY 14031
+1 16 759 2866

Right to the Moon Alice
240 Cooks Fall, Ithaca, NY 12776
+1 607 498 5750

Chicabow Ltd
218 Bedford Avenue, Brooklyn, NY
+1 718 599 6232

Hooti Couture
321 Flatbush Avenue, Brooklyn, NY
11217-2833
+1 718 857 1977
www.hooticouture.com
Alison Houtte, who bears a striking resemblance to Ali MacGraw, owns this

The Family Jewels

Where? 130 West 23rd Street, Manhattan, New York, NY 10011
+1 212 633 6020
www.familyjewelsnyc.com

Why go there? For 20 years, it's had a reputation as 'America's best vintage shop'. Set in the heart of Chelsea, it is visited by all the top American designers. One of the few vintage stores to enjoy an impressive level of media coverage in *Vanity Fair*, *Interview*, *Vogue* and *Elle*.

What's it like? With jazzy sounds floating through the store, Family Jewels offers a little calm in the midst of crazy busy New York. There is an old-world charm to the way the shop is laid out and the staff potter around the store as though in the comfort of their home where you are a very welcomed guest. Clothes are separated by era and style. One particularly sparkly rail features heavily sequined sweaters, another has an array of printed Seventies' dresses. The front of the shop showcases a wonderful display of Victorian blouses and wedding dresses, costume jewellery and an eclectic section of menswear. Never mind that there is a lot to take in. Family Jewels have clearly taken this into consideration. In addition to the assortment of clothing, there is a squishy leopard-print sofa and chairs where you can take a break from the rigours of shopping.

Best for? Fabulous dresses spanning every decade, Lucite bags, beaded purses, cool menswear, swimwear and Victorian blouses.

Clientele? Stylists, tourists, fashionable New Yorkers and little old ladies with a great sense of style.

Hot Tip? During summer and other holiday seasons, they hold great sales. This is a good place to shop for menswear, but if you're with a particularly tall man, tell him to mind his head. The ceiling is very low.

Prices? Fur capes at $175 are pricey in comparison to other places, but there are still some bargains – a fantastic Prada-esque dress at $39.

Flatbush-based vintage store. As she used to be a model for Karl Lagerfeld, Yohji Yamamoto and Azzedine Alaïa, her knowledge of fashion is extensive. Hooti stocks a fantastic range of jewellery (from $20), Fifties' cocktail dresses, fur stoles and croc skin and other styles of handbags (from $18–$300). Visit for the friendly one-to-one atmosphere while mixing with a wide range of customers, including the ghetto fabulous, Japanese tourists and many fashion designers' right-hand men.

Lady Bird

136 Bedford Avenue, Brooklyn,
NY 11211
+1 718 599 9300

The 1909 Company

63 Thompson Street, Manhattan,
New York, NY 10012
+1 212 343 1658

A Girl's Habit

17 Bleeker Street, Manhattan,
New York, NY 10012
+1 212 473 8465

Alice Underground

481 Broadway, Manhattan, New York,
NY 10012
+1 212 431 9067

Amarcord

84 East 7th Street, Manhattan,
New York NY
+1 212 614 7133

Atomic Passion

430 East 9th Street, Manhattan,
New York, NY 10009
+1 212 533 0718

This store is a one-stop destination for the shoe obsessed. There is an amazing assortment of footwear here – literally wall-to-wall coverage. A pair of Dior brown croc shoes, $85, and a Courrèges patent red wedge heels, $240, dwell quite happily with a 1900 pair of battered leather lace-up boots, $235. For those on the hunt for clothing, Atomic Passion doesn't disappoint. A pink Twenties' silk dress with an attached cape was on sale for $120, a printed Gunne Sax dress, $85, and a Fifties' navy blue eyelet dress, $125. Never mind that the décor is a little kitsch – Christmas type decorations hang from the ceiling all year round – and the owners Gigi and Justin are completely covered in tattoos. Regardless of the other distractions, this is a fabulous place to shop.

DIRECTORY

Cherry
18 Eighth Avenue, Manhattan,
New York, NY 10014
+1 212 924 1410
www.cherryboutique.com

Cherry Resource Center
Long Island City, NY
+1 212 924 1410
www.cherryboutique.com
Those with a penchant for shoes from the glamorous eras of yesteryear will be in seventh heaven. This New York relatively new hunting ground houses the world's largest collection of pristine, unworn vintage shoes. The footwear all come in their original boxes and viewing them within the mammoth warehouse is absolutely breathtaking – up to 80,000 of them are displayed floor to ceiling, classified by size, style and colour. Also stock a large range of vintage bags and some clothing and furniture. Visit by appointment only.

David Owens Vintage Clothing
154 Orchard Street, Manhattan,
New York, NY 10002
+1 212 677 3301

Deco Jewels
131 Thompson Street, Manhattan,
New York, NY 10012
+1 212 253 1222

Ellen Christine Millinery
255 West 18th Street, Manhattan,
New York, NY 10011
+1 212 242 2457

Eye Candy
329 Lafayette Street, Manhattan,
New York, NY 10012
+1 212 343 4275

Harriet Love
126 Prince Street, Manhattan,
New York, NY 10012
+1 212 966 2280

Jana Starr Antique
236 East 80th Street, Ground Floor,
Manhattan, New York, NY 10021
+1 212 861 8256

Keni Valenti
247 West 30th Street, 5th Floor,
Manhattan, New York NY
+1 212 967 7147

Live Shop Die
151 Avenue A, Manhattan,
New York, NY 10009
+1 212 674 7265

Lorraine Wohl Collection
860 Lexington Avenue, Manhattan,
New York, NY 10021
+1 212 472 0191

I think the most successful vintage stores are run by people with amazing taste – **if the owner or buyer doesn't have a good unusual eye then the store itself means nothing**. *My favourite collectors are Stephen Phillip at Rellik, London, not only does he have an excellent eye but he has a fascinating fashion education – he really loves British fashion – so his knowledge of Westwood, Hardy Amies, Galliano, John Flett, Bodymap, Pam Hogg, Rifat Ozbek is all excellent. Keni Valenti in New York is brilliant too – completely New Yorky, loud, mouthy and you just know this man has lived the club scene – and his taste reflects that, he has brilliant collections of the American designers – Stephen Sprouse, Giorgio di Sant'Angelo, Halston, in addition he has good vintage pieces from Gucci, Celine (really overlooked) and Rudi Geinrich. Shannon at New York Vintage is also brilliant, she has the most unusual taste ranging from Victorian costume pieces through to Adrian, YSL, Chanel and Balenciaga. All her pieces are amazingly restored, she also has really beautiful taste in handbags and jewellery. Cassie Mercantile is my other favourite, this time for menswear. His taste in military/army pieces and American sportswear is really excellent, he also has really lovely bags and belts. Which particular pieces or designers do I see as future collectables?* **I'm sure that Vivienne Westwood will continue to be collectable – along with Comme des Garçons, Yohji, Balenciaga, Chanel – I suppose the same designers that have always been highly desired**. *I think the quality of garments will be appreciated in future years – the make and finish on Prada, Marc Jacobs and Lanvin will be hugely referenced in years to come – making the pieces very collectable – the same as designers tend to look to vintage Chanel, Dior and Balenciaga now.*

KATIE GRAND
Stylist for *Prada* and *Miu Miu* and Editor, *Pop Magazine*

DIRECTORY

Lucille Antique Emporium
127 West 26th Street, Manhattan,
New York, NY 10001
+1 212 691 1041

Marmalade
172 Ludlow Street, Manhattan,
New York, NY 10002
+1 212 473 8030

Mary Efron Vintage
68 Thompson Street, Manhattan,
New York, NY 10012
+1 212 219 3099

O Mistress Mine
143 7th Avenue South, Manhattan,
New York, NY 10014
+1 212 691 4327

Oldies Goodies & Moldies
1609 Second Avenue, Manhattan,
New York, NY 10028
+1 212 737 3935

Oly's Vintage
210 East 21st Street, Manhattan,
New York, NY
+1 212 673 2800

Patricia Pastor Vintage
24 East 82nd Street, Manhattan,
New York, NY 10028
+1 212 734 4673

Reminiscence
50 West 23rd Street, Manhattan,
New York, NY 10014
+1 212 243 2292

Resurrection
217 Mott Street, Manhattan,
New York, NY 10012
+1 212 625 1374

Rose is Vintage
96 East 7th Street, Manhattan,
New York, NY 10009
+1 212 533 8550

Screaming Mimi's
382 Lafayette Street, Manhattan,
New York, NY 10003
+1 212 677 6464
Screaming Mimi's is a mix of kitsch and couture. It's one of the few stores you'll find Balenciaga, Pucci, Cardin and Yves Saint Laurent pieces hanging out with more throwaway Sixties' polyester dresses and Eighties' Iron Maiden badges. Prices are therefore extreme. A Seventies' towelling sundress can cost $50 while upstairs over the couture section a Rudi Gernreich black pleated dress with gold trim will cost nearly $800. You can also buy original copies of *Interview* magazine by special negotiation. Also has a Tokyo branch 18-4 Daikanyama-Cho, ShibuyaKu, Tokyo, Japan 150, +03 780 4415

Southpaw Vintage
226 West 37th Street, 8th Floor,
Manhattan, New York, NY 10018
+1 212 244 2768

Star Struck
47 Greenwich Avenue, Manhattan,
New York, NY 10014
+1 212 691 5357

Stella Dallas
218 Thompson Street, Manhattan,
New York, NY 10014
+1 212 674 0447

Village Scandal
19 East 7th Street, Manhattan,
New York, NY 10009
+1 212 460 9358

Vintage Clothes by Rue Saint Denis
174 Avenue B (at 11th Ave),
Manhattan, New York, NY 10009
+1 212 260 3388

What Goes Around Comes Around
351 West Broadway, Manhattan,
New York, NY 10013
+1 212 343 9303

Time Warp
124 Jay Street, Suite 222,
Schenectady, NY 12305
+1 518 347 1126

Ricky's Place
274 Goodman's Street, South
Rochester, NY 14607
+1 716 442 0042

Vintage 2000
4 Wall Street, Huntington, Suffolk
County, Long Island, NY 11743
+1 631 385 7070

Vintage by Stacy Lee
305 Central Avenue, Suite 4,
White Plains, NY 10606
+1 914 328 0788

—North Carolina

Time After Time
414 West Franklin Street,
Chapel Hill, NC 27514
+1 919 942 2304

Everything but Granny's Panties
2926 Guess Road, Durham,
NC 27705
+1 919 471 0996

Untidy Museum
2007 Chapel Hill Road, Durham,
NC 27707
+1 919 419 8841

I'm a huge fan of thrift stores in New York. *I don't follow any particular rules and therefore my taste is pretty varied – I really like Norma Kamali, strange unusual belts and I own a fantastic beautifully old Dior Cape from the Seventies.* **I just love what I love.** *So for anyone new to buying vintage clothing, I would say, think about which pieces fit in with what you already have and use your imagination.* **It's more about developing as opposed to changing your personal style.**

BAY GARNETT
Stylist, Fashion Consultant for
Matthew Williamson, TopShop and *Chloé*
and Founding Editor of thrift fashion
magazine *Cheap Date*

Old Habits Vintage Boutique
3012 Hillsborough Street, Raleigh,
NC 27607
+1 919 833 2747

—North Dakota

Make Believe Room
2500 Demers Avenue, Grand Forks,
ND 58201
+1 701 772 1922

—Ohio

Casablanca Vintage
3944 Spring Grove Avenue,
Cincinnati, OH 45223
+1 513 541 06999
This huge store claims to have the
largest selection of vintage clothing in
Cincinnati. One floor is totally dedicated
to sales while the other is for rental
purposes. You can find clothes from
every decade right up the Eighties.

Down Town Nostalgic
119 Calhoun Street, Cincinnati,
OH 45219
+1 513 861 9336

Edie's House of Vintage
3233 Harrison Avenue, Cincinnati,
OH 45211
+1 513 662 3700

Gayle's Vintage Clothing
3742 Kelogg Avenue, Cincinnati,
OH 45226
+1 513 321 7341

Talk of the Town
9111 Reading Road, Cicinnati,
OH 45215
+1 513 563 8844

Chelsea's Vintage Clothing
1412 West 116th Street, Cleveland,
OH 44102
+1 216 226 9147

Cleveland Shop
11606 Detroit Avenue, Cleveland,
OH 44102
+1 216 228 9725

Legacy Antiques & Vintage
12502 Larchmere Boulevard,
Cleveland, OH 44120
+1 216 229 0578

Lorain Suite Antiques & Interiors
7105 Lorain Avenue, Cleveland,
OH 44102
+1 216 281 1959
Suite Lorain is an incredible 8,000
square feet vintage emporium that is
now a Cleveland institution. Stocks
pieces from the Forties up to the
Seventies. Particularly brilliant for
Bakelite jewellery. Frequented by

vintage dealers, fashion stylists and customers from all over the US.

Renaissance Parlour
18381/2 Coventry Road, Cleveland, OH 44118
+1 216 932 8840

Kathryn's Quality Vintage Bridal Gowns
1247 North High Street, Columbus, OH 43201
+1 614 299 7923

Nostalgia Vintage Clothing
1200 North High Street, Columbus, OH 43201
+1 614 421 1930

Dorothy's Vintage Boutique
521 East 5th Street, Dayton, OH 45402
+1 937 461 7722

Feather's Vintage Clothing
440 East 5th Street, Dayton, OH 45402
+1 937 228 2940

It's in the Past
3706 Windyhollow Way, Mason, OH 45040
+1 513 339 0354

Stitches in Time
6 East Main Street, Plymouth, OH 44865
+1 419 687 2061

—Oklahoma

Peeka Boo Teck
308 1/2 Northwest 1st Street, Anadarko, OK 73005
+1 405 247 6615

Jean's Vintage Clothing
6812 Northwest 22nd Street, Bethany, OK 73008
+1 405 789 3252

Miss Sarah's Antiques
201 East Main Street, Davis, OK 73030
+1 580 369 2092

Ivy Cottage & Rose Garden
622 SW D Avenue, Lawton, OK 73501
+1 580 248 8768

Vintage Vibe
311 West Main Street, Norman, OK 73069
+1 405 447 4777

Collectibles Etc
1511 North Meridian, Oklahoma City,
OK 73107
+1 405 524 1700

Sparkle Plenty Vintage Clothing
918 West Britton Road, Oklahoma
City, OK 73114
+1 405 842 0905

Top Hat Vintage Clothing
4411 North Western Avenue,
Oklahoma City, OK 73118
+1 405 557 1732

Vintage Plus
727 Northwest 23rd Street,
Oklahoma City, OK 73103
+1 405 524 0086

—Oregon

Renaissance Rose
33 North Main Street, Ashland,
OR 97520
+1 541 488 0119

Persona Vintage Clothing & Antiques
100 10th Street, Astoria, OR 97103
+1 503 325 3837

Nobody's Baby
365 East 13th Avenue, Eugene,
OR 97401
+1 541 343 6842

Putting On the Ritz
350 East 11th Avenue, Eugene,
OR 97401
+1 541 686 9240

Cheap Thrills Eclectic Boutique
575 Highway 101, Florence,
OR 97439
+1 541 902 0187

Lavenders Green Historic Clothing
Hillsboro, OR
+1 503 640 6936

Perry & Delia's Vintage Clothing
10613 Southeast Main, Milwaukee,
OR
+1 503 786 8743

Decades Vintage Company
328 Southwest Stark Street,
Portland, OR 97204
+1 503 223 1177

Grand Funke Vintage
1925 Northeast 42nd Avenue,
Suite D, Portland, OR 97213
+1 503 282 6085

Hatties Vintage
2721 Southeast 26th Avenue,
Portland, OR 97202
+1 503 235 5305

279

DIRECTORY

Ray's Ragtime
*1021 Southwest Morrison Street,
Portland, OR 97205*
+1 503 226 2616

Reflections in Time
*1114 North West 21st, Portland,
OR 97209*
+1 503 223 7880

Torso Vintages Oddities & Collectibles
*2424 North West Broadway Street,
Portland, OR 97232*
+1 503 281 7232

Vintage Clothing
*10613 Southeast Main Street,
Portland, OR 97222*
+1 503 786 8743

Vintage Dress
*8425 Southeast 13th Street,
Portland, OR*
+1 503 231 7798

—Pennsylvania

Altoonafish
*1402 1/2 11th Avenue, Altoona,
PA 16601*
+1 814 944 2056

S&R Treasures
*332 North Queen Street, Lancaster,
PA 17603*
+1 717 299 1676

Zap & Co
*315 North Queen Street, Lancaster,
PA*
+1 717 397 7405

Fairy Godmother's
*13 West Main Street, Mechanicsburg,
PA*
+1 717 795 8100

Night Owl Vintage Clothing
*10 Stockton Avenue, New Hope,
PA 18938*

Antiquarian's Delight
*615 South 6th Street, Philadelphia,
PA 19147*
+1 215 592 0256

Ballyhoo
*230 North Second Street,
Philadelphia, PA 19106*
+1 215 627 1700

Decaddes Vintage
*1511 South Street, Philadelphia,
PA 19146*
+1 215 483 1579

Decaddes Vintage
4369 Cresson Street, Philadelphia,
PA 19127
+1 215 483 1579

Past & Present
7224 Germantown Avenue,
Philadelphia, PA 19119
+1 215 242 2908

Pennyfeathers
1312 South Street, Philadelphia,
PA 19147
+1 215 772 1945

Eons Fashion Antique
5850 Ellsworth Avenue, Pittsburgh,
PA 15232
+1 412 361 3368

Yesterday's News
1405 East Carson Street, Pittsburgh,
PA 15203
+1 412 431 1712

Another Time
49 North Main Street, Shrewsbury,
PA 17361
+1 717 235 0664

Memories
622 Penn Avenue, Sinking Spring,
PA 19608
+1 610 374 4480

Barbara Kennedy
125 West Lawn Avenue, West Lawn,
PA 19609
+1 610 796 7303

The Cat's Pajamas
335 Maynard Street, Williamsport,
PA 17701
+1 570 322 5580

—Rhode Island

Artifice
307 Main Street, East Greenwich,
RI 02818
+1 401 734 9920

Rag & Bone Vintage Clothing
346 Atwells Avenue, Providence,
RI 02903
+1 401 397 3076

Ragtime
180 Angell Street, Providence, RI
+1 401 521 7140

Diva's Palace
334 Knight Street, Suite 1,
Warwick, RI 02886
+1 401 739 0918

Lois Hollingsworth
53 South Atlantic Avenue, Warwick,
RI 02888
+1 401 461 7306

Obviously, you're buying vintage for the love of it. But it can be a wise investment buy as well. Some labels hold their value better than others: Chanel, for example, tends only ever to increase in value, especially if the piece is in pristine condition. **Karl Lagerfeld's legwarmers apart, nearly all Chanel is a future classic***: the boucle jacket might change superficially each season, but it is still an iconic item. If you invest in one, you might retire it for a season or so, but you will always come back to it. Sellers know this, which is why prices are always so high.* **Pucci is another label which increases in value. The older or rarer the prints, the more of a collector's item they will be***. Ditto Vivienne Westwood and John Galliano: if you bought any in the Eighties, it will be worth a small fortune now. I have a shredded denim jacket from Westwood's Pirate collection which, to be honest, makes me look like a stonewashed chicken. I've only worn it once, but I still retain it because it's a wonderful piece. Maybe it will be my pension when I'm old and grey. As for future classics – well, now that Phoebe Philo has resigned from Chloé anything from her four-year tenure will be extra-collectable. Ditto any Tom Ford for Gucci (more than Tom Ford for YSL, I'd say), although his tenure was longer and therefore his designs less rare. Also anything by Nicolas Ghesquière for Balenciaga: his clothes are manufactured in such small quantities that they are hard to find even now, never mind in 20 years. And of course, anything by Rei Kawakubo for the sheer craftsmanship. Ditto Hermès: a bluechip brand whose value will always endure thanks to its extraordinary levels of craftsmanship.*

LAURA CRAIK
Fashion editor, *Evening Standard* and *Grazia*

Granny's Goodies

Where? 310 King Street,
Charleston, South Carolina, 29401
(843) 577 6200

Why go there? This long-standing vintage clothing shop is widely known as one of the best vintage stores in Charleston. So much so that clients will quite happily travel for miles to pay a visit.

What's it like? Small, charming and very Southern, as you would expect a vintage store in the heart of the Deep South to be. Run by a couple that treat each customer as a returning friend, offering practical advice and friendly recommendations.

Best for? Although their stock ranges from the Twenties, the bulk of Granny's pieces are across the Forties to the Seventies.

Clientele? The college girl looking for a one-off prom night frock, the cool vintage aficionado, the nostalgic pensioner eager to step back in time... This store is such a landmark that it is frequented by a vast array of people. Local arty types – particularly musicians and artists – also love it. A recent exhibition showcased the end results of the store donating 30 vintage suitcases to artists, giving them free reign to do with the cases as they pleased.

Hot tip? Their opening times are pretty erratic so ring before you head out there. You can also sell your own pieces through Granny's Goodies but need to make an appointment before hand.

Prices? Pretty inexpensive. Many pieces start around the $25 mark.

DIRECTORY

—South Dakota

Second Impression Palace
412 North Main Street, Mitchell,
SD 57301
+1 605 996 1948

Worth Repeating
103 East Kemp, Watertown,
SD 57201
+1 605 882 4734

—Tennessee

Dee's Vintage Shop
1205 North Central Street,
Knoxville, TN 37917
+1 865 637 9030

Legacy
117 South Central Street, Knoxville,
TN 37902
+1 865 523 7335

Flashback
2304 Central Avenue, Memphis,
TN 38104
+1 901 272 2304

Vintage Mania
2151 Young Avenue, Memphis,
TN 38104
+1 901 274 2879

Retro Pieces
211 Louise Avenue, Nashville,
TN 37203
+1 615 329 3537

Silvery Moon
207 Louise Avenue, Nashville,
TN 37203
+1 615 329 9003

Venus & Mars
2830 Bransford Avenue, Nashville,
TN 37204
+1 615 269 8357

Zelda
5133 Harding Road, Nashville,
TN 37205
+1 615 356 2430

—Texas

Amelia's Retro Vogue & Relics
2024 South Lamar Boulevard
Austin, TX 78704
+1 512 442 4446

Big Bertha's Bargain Basement
1050 South Lamar Boulevard,
Austin, TX 78704
+1 512 444 5908

Champagne Clotheshorse/Kimono
1030 South Lamar Boulevard,
Austin, TX 78704
+1 512 441 9955

Flashback
2047 South Lamar Boulevard,
Austin, TX 78704
+1 512 445 6906

Hog Wild
100 East North Loop Boulevard,
Austin, TX 78751
+1 512 467 9453

Ivory Aisles (wedding dresses)
2032 South Lamar Boulevard
Austin, TX 78704
+1 512 444 6484

Lets Dish
1102 South Lamar Boulevard,
Austin, TX 78704
+1 512 444 9801

Old Time Teenies Vintage Clothing
11261/2 West 6th Street, Austin,
TX 78703
+1 512 477 2022

Rock Island Line
215 West North Loop Boulevard,
Austin, TX
+1 512 445 6906

Ahab Bowen
2614 Boll Street, Dallas, TX 75204
+1 214 720 1874
A long-time favourite with the locals, this shop specialises in fashions that span the Forties, Fifties, Sixties and Seventies. Considering its downtown location, prices are still very reasonable. Look out for their sales where you can pick up brilliant bargains. Voted best vintage shop in Texas many times over.

Puttin On the Ritz
6615 Snider Plaza, Dallas,
TX 75205
+1 214 369 4015

Bon Ton Vintage Clothing
Forreston Vintage Market, Highway
77 at Main, Forreston, TX 76041
+1 972 483 6222
Bon Ton's two floors are filled with vintage fashions from 1900 to 1970, books and works of arts. All the clothing is in great condition and there are a lot of deadstock pieces to choose from. Women can indulge in dainty dresses and cocktail hats while men peruse over the extensive range of old military uniforms.

DIRECTORY

Vintage Oasis
1512 Westheimer Road, Houston,
TX 77006
+1 713 529 2234

The Way We Wore
2602 Waugh Drive, Houston,
TX 77006
+1 713 526 8910

JAI
919 South Alamo Street,
San Antonio, TX 78205
+1 210 225 4272

Nelda's Vintage Clothing
1621 North Main Avenue,
San Antonio, TX 78212
+1 210 271 7111

Vintage Closet
5223 McCullough Avenue,
San Antonio, TX 78212
+1 210 824 6222

Revivals Inc
222 West Front Street, Tyler,
TX 75702
+1 903 597 2229

Blast from the Past
1801 Fort Avenue, Waco, TX 76707
+1 254 714 1183

—Utah

Vintage a la Vogue
2 West Saint George Boulevard,
Saint George, UT 84770
+1 435 673 4897

Antiques Gallery
217 East 300 South, Salt Lake City,
UT
+1 801 521 7055

Arsenic & Old Lace / Briar Patch
Antiques
407 East 300 South, Salt Lake City,
UT
+1 801 322 5234

Garps Mercantile
627 South State Street, Salt Lake
City, UT 84111
+1 801 537 1357

Grunts & Postures
779 East 300 South, Salt Lake City,
84102
+1 801 521 3202

—Vermont

Battery Street Jeans
182 Battery Street, Burlington,
VT 05401
+1 802 865 6223

Rainments & Adornment
Main Street, South Stafford, VT
+1 802 765 4335

Karen Augusta
33 Gage Street North, Westminster,
VT 05101
+1 802 463 3333

Who is Sylvia?
26 Central Street, Woodstock,
VT 05091
+1 802 457 1110

—Virginia

Funk & Junk
106 1/2 North Columbus Street
Alexandria, VA 22314
+1 703 836 0749

Vintage Fiber Works
1200 Main Street, Lynchburg,
VA 24504
+1 804 845 3601

Bygones Vintage Clothing
2916 West Cary Street, Richmond,
VA 23221
+1 804 353 1919

Exile
822 West Grace Street, Richmond,
VA 23220
+1 804 358 3348

Halcyon Vintage Clothing
117 North Robinson Street,
Richmond, VA 23220
+1 804 358 1311

Luxor Vintage
3001 West Cary Street, Richmond,
VA 23221
+1 804 359 6780

—Washington

Blue Moon Vintage Clothing
214 West Holly Street, Bellingham,
WA 98225
+1 360 752 2789

Doubletake Vintage
1175 Northwest Gilman Boulevard,
Suite B6, Issaquah, WA 98027
+1 425 392 4908

Retroville Vintage Outfitters
133 East First Street, Port Angeles,
WA 98362
+1 360 452 1429

Fritzi Ritz Vintage Clothing
3425 Fremont Place, North Seattle,
WA 98103
+1 206 633 0929

DIRECTORY

Isadora Antique Clothing
1915 1st Avenue, Seattle,
WA 98101
+1 206 441 7711

Madame & Co
1901 10th Avenue, West Seattle,
WA 98119
+1 206 281 7908

Private Screening
3504 Fremont Place, North Seattle,
WA 98103
+1 206 548 0751

Red Light
312 Broadway, East Seattle,
WA 98102
+1 206 329 2200

Rudy's Vintage Clothing
1424 1st Avenue, Seattle,
WA 98101
+1 206 682 6586

Vintage Voola
705 East Pike Street, Seattle,
WA 98122
+1 206 324 2808

OBO Collectibles
1604 West Riverside Avenue,
Spokane, WA 99201
+1 509 838 5017

Glenna's Clothing
783 Broadway, Tacoma, WA 98402
+1 253 627 8501

—Washington D.C.

Deja Vintage
3005 M Street, Northwest
Washington, DC 20007
+1 202 337 7100

Meeps & Aunt Neensies
1520 U Street, Northwest
Washington, DC 20009
+1 202 265 6546

Mood Indigo
1214 U Street, Northwest
Washington, DC 20009
+1 202 265 6366

Sylvia's Vintage Shop
2102 18th Street, Northwest
Washington, DC 20009
+1 202 328 9882

—West Virginia

VaVavoom Retro
119 Pleasant Street, Morgantown,
WV 26505
+1 304 292 5505

I think the recent trend of wearing vintage clothing has been essential in revitalising the fashion business. It has taught us to respect those designers in the past who revolutionised the industry, and who now inspire the younger designers, who fully acknowledge the gift that they have been given by citing archive research whenever they can. **Personally, I love to wear vintage as much as possible - I usually mix it with the new.** There is that wonderful satisfaction that you will be wearing something completely individual and unique. I know a few women who wear solely vintage, but this truly needs an expert eye to get it right. These women have searched and researched, and always look incredible. It takes a lot of confidence, but they have the strength of mind to use vintage designs to embrace current trends by making them completely their own.

ALISON EDMOND
Creative Director, *Harpers Bazaar*

DIRECTORY

A Penny Saved Antique Mall
230 Main Avenue, Weston, WV
+1 304 269 4200

—Wisconsin

Dime a Dance
Cedar Creek Settlement, Cedarburg,
WI 53012
+1 262 377 5054

Red Shed Antiques
On County Highway B, Hayward, WI
+1 715 634 6088

Vintage Vogue
115 5th Avenue South, LaCrosse,
WI 54601
+1 608 782 3722

Florilegum
823 East Johnson Street, Madison,
WI 53703
+1 608 256 7310

Juju & Moxie
458 West Gilman Street, Madison,
WI 53703
+1 608 255 4002

Closet Classics
1531 North Farwell Avenue,
Milwaukee, WI 53202
+1 414 271 1950

Flapper Alley
1518 North Farwell Avenue,
Milwaukee, WI 53202
+1 414 276 6252

Marlene's Touch of Class
249 North Water Street, Milwaukee,
WI 53202
+1 414 272 2470

Orchid Annies
1327 East Brady Street, Milwaukee,
WI 53202
+1 414 347 0606

Everything Vintage at Isaac's Antique
Mall
132 East Main Street, Mount Horeb,
WI 53572
+1 608 437 6151

• *other* **Vintage** SOURCES

Vintage fairs

United Kingdom

—England

The Battersea Vintage Fashion Fair
Battersea Arts Centre, Lavender Hill,
London SW11
+44 (0)20 8325 5789

Frock Me!
Chelsea Town Hall, Kings Road,
London SW3
+44 (0)20 7254 4054

The London Vintage Fashion, Textiles and Accessories Fair
Hammersmith Town Hall, King Street
London W6
+44 (0)20 8543 5075
www.pa-antiques.co.uk
Paola Francia Gardiner prides herself on being the one who introduced the phrase 'vintage clothing' to the world of 'period clothing'. She now runs one of the most successful vintage fairs in the country. Launched in 1999, this Hammersmith-based fair features over 100 top vintage dealers from across the country. A vintage lover's dream, the pieces go way past second-hand or retro and fall securely into the 'proper vintage' category. Majority of these traders don't have a shop, while some operate only via the internet so this is fantastic way to gain access to otherwise elusive clothing. Highlights on offer include an Ossie Clark / Celia Birtwell dress for £375, a pale green Grecian-style sequinned dress for £35, an exquisite Fifties' carpet bag for £10 a Jean Varon dress for £175, an Art Deco silver Twenties' dress for £495, a petrol blue and gold-trimmed Janice Wainwright dress for £95 and a Leonard piece for the same price. As the title suggests, it isn't just clothing that is available to buy here. You can buy anything from delicate Edwardian fabrics to 1975 copies of *Vogue*. With textiles and clothing spanning all decades and prices to suit all pockets, it comes as no surprise that this vintage fair is a source of inspiration for both fashion designers and students. Prices will obviously differ from one dealer to another however don't be afraid to haggle, as this is totally expected and acceptable. Cash and cheques are the main forms of payment accepted – but as there are so many 'goodies ' on offer, your best bet is to set yourself a realistic budget and stick to it, as this must be the easiest place in the world to overspend.

Vintage Modes
The Music Room, Grays Antique Market, 26 South Molton Lane, London W1
+44 (0)20 7629 7043

Passion for Fashion
Sotheby's Fashion and Textiles Auction, Kerry Taylor
07785 734 337
www.sothebys.com
Initially set up as an in-house fashion collectors' department in 1985, Sotheby's Passion for Fashion sales are now run out of house by Kerry Taylor Auctions twice a year. Taylor herself travels all over the world meeting collectors who want to sell their treasures. The items featured in the sale of course are very much dependent on what clients are selling. In the past Taylor has sold a huge collection of Madeleine Vionnet dresses discovered in an old French house, Hermes bags from the Sixties and Seventies estimated at anything from £600 to £3,000, Ossie Clark dresses estimated at £300, a Charles Worth satin and velvet ball gown estimated between £400 and £600. She has sold collections from the Duke and Duchess of Windsor, Princess Lillian of Belgium (mainly Dior and Balenciaga pieces worn only once) and Romilly McAlpine. Most pieces are sold not much more than the estimated prices. This auction attracts a variety of buyers from the established designers looking for inspiration to the curious shopper looking for a new way to shop for vintage clothing. A good way to buy a high quality piece at a fair price – fair because, of course, the price is dictated by demand.

United States

—California

The Vintage Fashion Expo
+1 707 793 0773
www.vintagessilhouette.com

—Chicago

Chicago Vintage Clothing & Antique Textile Show & Sale
www.dolphinfairs.com

—Connecticut

Greater Hartford Vintage Clothing & Jewellery Show & Sale
+1 860 342 2540

Vintage Clothing, Estate & Costume Jewellery Expo
+1 914 248 4646

DIRECTORY

—Massachusetts

Antique Textiles, Vintage Fashions
Show & Sale
www.vintagefashionandtextileshow.com

—New York

The NYC Metropolitan Vintage
Fashion & Antique Textile Show
and Sale
+1 212 463 0200
www.newyorkvintagefashionshow.com

The Manhattan Vintage Clothing Store
www.ekinesis.com/manhattanvintage

NYC Triple Pier Expo
www.stellashows.com

Vintage Clothing, Estate & Costume
Jewellery Expo
www.mavenscompany.com

—Tennessee

International Vintage Textile Show
+1 317 722 9016

—Texas

Victorian Elegance
www.victorianshow.com

—Canada

The Clothing Show
*100 Princes' Boulevard (Automotive
Building), Toronto, ON M6K 3C3*
+1 416 657 2156
www.theclothingshow.com

Vintage show organisers

—United States

Caskey Lees
PO Box 1409, Topanga, CA 90290
+1 310 455 2886

Cat's Pajamas
*125 West Main Street, W, Dundee,
IL 60118*
+1 847 428 8368

Deco to 50s
*1217 Waterview Drive, Mill Valley,
CA 94941*
+1 415 383 3008

Eileen Love
+1 914 988 9609

J.R. Promotions
+1 509 375 5273

Maven Company
+1 914 248 4646

Metropolitan Art & Antiques
125 West 18th Street, New York,
NY 10011
+1 212 463 0200

Oldies But Goodies
Hankins, NY
+1 914 887 5272

Show Associates
PO Box 729, Cape Neddick,
ME 03902
+1 207 439 2334

Stella Show Management
147 West 24th Street, New York,
NY 10011
+1 212 255 0020

The Williamsburg Vintage Fashion &
Accessories Show
+1 215 862 5828

Vintage Expo
+1 707 793 0773

—United Kingdom

PA Antiques
+44 (0)20 8543 5075
www.pa-antiques.co.uk

Pre-empt Events
16 Garden Road, Bromley BR1 3LX
+44 (0)20 8290 1888
www.vintagefashionfairs.com

Flea markets

—United Kingdom

The Car Boot and Market Calendar
PO Box 277, Hereford HR2 9AY
+44 (0)1981 251633
www.carbootcalendar.com

—United States

http://fleamarket.directoryusa.biz/ind
ex.php

Auction houses

—Australia

Lawson – Menzies
212 Cumberland Street, Sydney,
NSW 2000
+61 2 9241 3411
www.lawson-menzies.com

—France

Drouot Richelieu
15, Avenue Montaigne, Paris 75008
+33 1 48 00 20 80

Galerie Charpentier
76, rue du Faubourg Saint-Honoré,
Paris 75008
+33 1 53 05 53 05

—United Kingdom

Bonhams
101 New Bond Street,
London W1S 1S
+44 (0)20 7447 7447
www.bonhams.com

Sotheby's
34–35 New Bond Street,
London W1A 2AA
+44 (0)20 7293 5000
www.sothebys.com

—United States

Christie's
20 Rockefeller Plaza, New York,
NY 10020
+1 212 636 2000
www.christies.com

Doyle's
175 East 87th Street, New York
NY 00
+1 212 427 2730
www.doylenewyork.com

Sotheby's
1334 New York Avenue at 72nd
Street, New York
+1 212 606 7000
www.sothebys.com

Wescheler's
909 East Street, N.W, Washington,
D.C. 20004
+1 202 628 1281

Charles Whittaker Auctions
7105 Emlen Street, Philadelphia,
PA 19119
+1 215 844 8788
www.whitakerauction.com

Vintage publications

Vintage!
Publication of Federation of Vintage Fashion
+1 707 793 0773

Vintage Gazette
Published by Molly Turner,
194 Amity Street, Amerherst,
MA 010002
+1 413 549 6446

Vintage websites

1860–1960 One Hundred Years of Fashion & Accessories
www.1860-1960.com

Adorable Vintage Costume Jewelry
www.adorablevintagecostume jewelry.com

Another Time Vintage Apparel
www.anothertimevintageapparel.com

Antique and Vintage Dress Galley
www.antiquedress.com

Antique Lace & Fashion
www.antique-fashion.com

A Vintage Wedding
www.avintagewedding.com

Azillion Sparklz
www.sparklz.com

Ballyhoo Vintage Clothing
www.ballyhoovintage.com

Britney and Me
www.britneyandme.com

Butterfly Vintage Clothing
www.butterflyvintage.com

C20 Vintage Fashion
www.c20vintagefashion.co.uk

The Cats Pajamas
www.catspajamas.com

Chelsea Girl
www.chelsea-girl.com

Cookies Closet Vintage
www.cookiescloset.com

The Daisy Shop
www.daisyshop.com

Dandelion Vintage Clothing
www.dandelion-vintage.com

Davenport and Company
www.davenportandco.com

Dresshopnyc
www.dresshopnyc.com

DIRECTORY

eBay
www.ebay.com

Enokiworld
www.enokiworld.com

The Fainting Couch
www.faintingcouch.com

Farley Enterprises
www.farley.com

FashionDig.com
www.fashiondig.com

Fever Vintage
www.fevervintage.com

The Frock.Com
www.thefrock.com

Glad Rags
www.vintagegladrags.com

Go Antiques
www.goantiques.com

Hemlock Vintage
www.hemlockvintage.com

Hey Viv!
www.heyviv.com

Ichiroya- Kimono Flea Market
www.ichiroya.com

Incongneeto Vintage
www.neetstuff.com

It's in the Past Vintage Clothing
www.itsinthepast.com

Jabot's Vintage Authentic
www.geocites.com/Eureka/Park/5956

Jewel Fever.com
www.jewelfever.com

Justsaywhen
www.justsaywhen.com

K8ty Kat
www.k8tykat.com

Kitty Girl Vintage
www.kittygirlvintage.com

La Pochette
www.lapochette.com

Lori Knowles
www.knowlesville.com

Miami Beach Vintage & Fashion
www.miamibeachvintage.com

Michelle's Vintage Jewellery
www.michellesvintagejewelry.com

Mid Century Chic
www.midcenturychic.com

Midnight Sparkle
www.tias.com/stores/midnightsparkle

ML Vintage
www.meredith.com.au

Nadia's Closet
www.nadiascloset.co.uk

Nancy's Nifty Nook Vintage Clothing
www.nancysniftynook.com

Neen's Antique & Vintage Clothing
www.neens.com

Nelda's Vintage Clothing
www.neldasvintageclothing.com

Paper Bag Princess
www.thepaperbagprincess.com

Persona Vintage
www.personavintage.com

Piece Unique
www.pieceunique.com

Polyesters
www.polyesters.net

POSH Vintage
www.poshvintage.com

Plush Vintage
www.plushvintage.com

Red Rose Vintage Clothing
www.rrnspace.com

Reflections of the Past
www.victoriana.com/antique-marketplace

Retrodress
www.retrodress.com

Rizzo's Reproduction Vintage Clothing
www.costumegallery.com

Ruby Lane
www.rubylane.com

Rusty Zipper
www.rustyzipper.com

Sazz Vintage Clothing
www.sazzvintage.com

Tangerine Boutique
www.tangerineboutique.com

The Old Lace and Linen Shop
www.antiquelinen.com

The Way We Were
www.the-way-we-were.com

The Way We Wore
www.thewaywewore.net

Trashy Diva
www.trashydiva.com

DIRECTORY

Truefax Vintage Costume Jewellery
www.truefaux.com

Ver Unica
www.ver-unica.com

Victorian Elegance
www.victorianelegance.com

Vintage and Lace
www.vintageandlace.com

Vintage Blues
www.vintageblues.com

Vintage Couture
www.vintagecouture.com

Vintage Glad Rags
www.vintagegladrags.com
Vintage Instyle
www.vintage-instyle.com

Vintage Kimono
www.vintagekimono.com

Vintage Textile
www.vintagetextile.com

Vintage Vixen Clothing Company
www.vintagevixen.com

Vintage Wedding
www.vintagewedding.com

Vintageous
www.vintageous.com

Viva La Frock
www.vivalafrock.co.uk

Viva La Vintage
www.vivalavintage.com

Wear it Again Sam
www.wearitagainsam.com

Wearable Vintage
www.wearablevintage.com

What Comes Around Goes Around
www.nyvintage.com

YOOX
www.yoox.com

International dress sizes

women

blouses	USA	32	34	36	38	40	42
	GB	6	8	10	12	14	16
	D	32	34	36	38	40	42
	F	34	36	38	40	42	44
	I	38	40	42	44	46	48
suits	USA	8	10	12	14	16	17
	GB	6	8	10	12	14	16
	D	32	34	36	38	40	42
	F	34	36	38	40	42	44
	I	38	40	42	44	46	48
shoes	USA	4 1/2	5 1/2	6 1/2	7 1/2	8 1/2	9 1/2
	GB	3	4	5	6	7	8
	D	36	37	38	39	40	41
	F	35	36	37	38	39	40
	I	36	37	38	39	40	41

men

shirts	USA	14	14 1/2	15 1/2	16 1/2	17 1/2	18 1/2
	GB	14	14 1/2	15 1/2	16 1/2	17 1/2	18 1/2
	D	38	40	42	44	46	48
	F	40	42	44	46	48	50
	I	44	46	48	50	52	54
suits	USA	36	38	40	42	44	46
	GB	36	38	40	42	44	46
	D	40	42	44	46	48	50
	F	42	44	46	48	50	52
	I	46	48	50	52	54	56
shoes	USA	7–7 1/2	8	9	10	11	12
	GB	6	7	8	9	10	11
	D	40	41	42	43	44	45
	F	40	41	42	43	44	45
	I	40	41	42	43	44	45

Editorial director Jane O'Shea
Creative director Helen Lewis
Designer Claire Peters
Project editor Lisa Pendreigh
Editorial assistant Andrew Bayliss
Illustrator Richard Merritt
Pictorial researcher Leanne Bracey
Research assistant Ejos Euribo
Production director Vincent Smith
Production controller Ruth Deary

Cover fabric supplied by Kona Bay
Fabrics, 2006 www.konabay.com
Title page fabric supplied by Kona
Bay Fabrics, 2005 www.konabay.com
Additional vintage fabrics supplied by
Katie Horwich

First published in 2007 by
Quadrille Publishing Limited
Alhambra House
27–31 Charing Cross Road
London WC2H 0LS
www.quadrille.co.uk

Reprinted in 2007
10 9 8 7 6 5 4 3 2

ISBN 978 184400 455 3

Printed and bound in China

All the information contained in this book
was correct at the time of going to press.
We would be happy to hear of any
amendments or omissions.
Please email enquiries@quadrille.co.uk